Higher ENGLISH **for CfE**

READING FOR UNDERSTANDING, ANALYSIS AND EVALUATION
ANSWERS AND MARKING SCHEMES

Ann Bridges and Colin Eckford

Although every effort has been made to ensure that website addresses are correct at time of going to press, Hodder Gibson cannot be held responsible for the content of any website mentioned in this book. It is sometimes possible to find a relocated web page by typing in the address of the home page for a website in the URL window of your browser.

Orders: please contact Bookpoint Ltd, 130 Park Drive, Abingdon, Oxon OX14 4SE. Telephone: (44) 01235 827720; Fax: (44) 01235 400454. Lines are open 9:00–5:00, Monday to Saturday, with a 24-hour message answering service. Visit our website at www.hoddereducation.co.uk. Hodder Gibson can be contacted direct on: Telephone: 0141 848 1609; Fax: 0141 889 6315; email: hoddergibson@hodder.co.uk

© Ann Bridges, Colin Eckford 2015

First published in 2015 by

Hodder Gibson, an imprint of Hodder Education,

An Hachette UK Company,

Carmelite House, 50 Victoria Embankment,

London EC4Y 0DZ

Impression number   5 4 3 2

Year   2019 2018 2017 2016 2015

All rights reserved. Apart from any use permitted under UK copyright law, no part of this publication may be reproduced or transmitted in any form or by any means, electronic or mechanical, including photocopying and recording, or held within any information storage and retrieval system, without permission in writing from the publisher or under licence from the Copyright Licensing Agency Limited. Further details of such licences (for reprographic reproduction) may be obtained from the Copyright Licensing Agency Limited, Saffron House, 6–10 Kirby Street, London EC1N 8TS.

Cover photo © contrastwerkstatt – Fotolia

Chapter opener image reproduced on pages 1, 2, 5, 9, 13, 16, 20, 24, 29, 34, 39, 44, 50 © contrastwerkstatt – Fotolia.

Typeset in Minion Regular 12/14.5 by Integra Software Services Pvt. Ltd., Pondicherry, India

Printed in Great Britain, by Hobbs the Printers Ltd, Totten, Hampshire, SO40 3WX

A catalogue record for this title is available from the British Library.

ISBN: 978 1 4718 4438 6

CONTENTS

Answers for questions in Part Two	1
Passage A Fracking	2
Passage B Gap years	5
Passage C Tattoos	9
Answers for questions in Part Three – Section 1	13
Exercise 1 Does man flu really exist?	13
Exercise 2 CCTV in schools	14
Exercise 3 JFK	14
Answers for questions in Part Three – Section 2	16
Exercise 4 The First World War	16
Exercise 5 Serving on a jury	16
Exercise 6 Competitive sport	18
Answers for questions in Part Three – Section 3	20
Exercise 7 Teenagers	20
Exercise 8 The importance of reading	21
Exercise 9 Sex education	22
Marking guidelines for Part Four	24
Paper 1 Homework	24
Paper 2 *Breaking Bad*	29
Paper 3 Conservation	34
Paper 4 Social networking	39
Paper 5 Christmas	44
Paper 6 Shopping	50

Answers for questions in Part Two

The Marking Guide for Part Two has been written to replicate the style of Marking Instructions used by SQA. This should help teachers/lecturers advise their students about the best way to answer and how marks will be allocated.

These detailed instructions can, and should, however, be used for more than simply marking students' responses – the additional points (especially in the questions calling for analysis) should be seen as a useful teaching tool. Exploring *all* the possible answers on word choice, sentence structure, and so on, is a very worthwhile classroom exercise for teachers and students alike.

Note: For ease of reference, the exact wording of each question is given, in bold, at the start of the relevant 'Expected response' column. This differs from SQA practice.

PASSAGE A – FRACKING

MARKING INSTRUCTIONS FOR EACH QUESTION

Question	Expected response	Max mark	Additional guidance
1.	**Explain in your own words the key points the writer makes in lines 1–13 about Scotland.** Candidates should explain the key points the writer makes about Scotland. Candidates must use their own words. No marks are awarded for verbatim quotations from the passage. *1 mark for each point from the 'Additional guidance' column.*	3	Possible answers include: • there are still visible signs of our industrial heritage • there has been a big change in recent years • the old industries have disappeared • a new way of thinking has emerged or any other acceptable answer.
2.	**Analyse how the writer's word choice in lines 14–20 conveys a positive image of Scotland.** Candidates should analyse how the writer's word choice conveys a positive image of Scotland. Marks will depend on the quality of comment on word choice. 2 marks may be awarded for reference plus detailed/insightful comment; 1 mark for reference plus more basic comment; 0 marks for reference alone. *Possible answers are shown in the 'Additional guidance' column.*	2	Possible answers include: • 'clean' suggests unspoiled, without the pollution of the industrial past • 'green' suggests natural, environmentally friendly • 'sustainable' suggests ecological, not destroying resources • 'beautiful' suggests attractive, appealing • 'unspoiled' suggests pristine, pure • 'rich' suggests abundance, profusion • 'leaders' suggests out in front, surpassing others' capabilities or any other acceptable answer.
3.	**Identify in your own words three advantages of fracking given in lines 21–31.** Candidates should identify in their own words three advantages of fracking. Candidates must use their own words. No marks are awarded for verbatim quotations from the passage. *1 mark for each point from the 'Additional guidance' column.*	3	Possible answers include: • it costs less than other sources of energy • the fuel it produces causes less damage to the environment • it will (by inference from USA) generate economic growth • it will (by inference from USA) generate employment or any other acceptable answer.
4.	**Identify in your own words three possible dangers of fracking given in lines 32–39.** Candidates should identify in their own words three possible dangers of fracking. Candidates must use their own words. No marks are awarded for verbatim quotations from the passage. *1 mark for each point from the 'Additional guidance' column.*	3	Possible answers include: • contamination of water • effect of carbon emissions on climate change • maintains our reliance on non-renewables • diverts our attention away from conservation and expansion of renewables or any other acceptable answer.

Answers for questions in Part Two

5.		**Explain why, according to lines 40–51, fracking is 'bound to seem tempting' to the Scottish Government.** Candidates should explain why fracking is 'bound to seem tempting' to the Scottish Government. Candidates must use their own words. No marks are awarded for verbatim quotations from the passage. *1 mark for each point from the 'Additional guidance' column.*	3	Possible answers include: • because it seems we have large amounts of resources ready to be exploited • because it will bring substantial economic benefits • because we have the know-how to exploit it • because it will reduce our reliance on energy from overseas • because the Government needs the money it will generate or any other acceptable answer.
6.	a)	**Re-read lines 52–60. Identify in your own words four advantages of renewable energy given in these lines.** Candidates should identify in their own words four advantages of renewable energy. Candidates must use their own words. No marks are awarded for verbatim quotations from the passage. *1 mark for each point from the 'Additional guidance' column.*	4	Possible answers include: • it encourages lower use of energy, discourages wastage • it causes less harm to the environment • it will not run out • Scotland has ideal resources (wind, tide, etc.) to make it work • it is forward-looking or any other acceptable answer.
6.	b)	**Re-read lines 52–60. Analyse how the writer's use of language in these lines emphasises the contrast between renewables and fracking.** Candidates should analyse how the writer's use of language emphasises the contrast between renewables and fracking. Marks will depend on the quality of comment. For full marks there must be at least one reference to each side of the contrast. 2 marks may be awarded for reference plus detailed/insightful comment; 1 mark for reference plus more basic comment; 0 marks for reference alone. Thus 4 marks could be gained as 2 + 2 or 2 + 1 + 1 or 1 + 1 + 1 + 1. *Possible answers are shown in the 'Additional guidance' column.*	4	Possible answers include: **Renewables:** • 'dream of the future' suggests an idealistic, positive view • 'infinitely attractive' suggests something almost immeasurably appealing • 'conserving' suggests taking care to preserve, protect • list ('better at … long-term future') suggests extensive benefits of renewables • 'green energy dream' suggests it will produce something highly desirable, is something to aspire to (if perhaps a little over-optimistic) • 'unique strengths' suggests renewables match up with something powerful and special in Scotland **Fracking:** • 'abandoning' suggests that adopting fracking would cause a serious loss • 'profligate' suggests that the use of fracking/non-renewables is inefficient, encourages wasteful behaviour • 'plunge' suggests that embracing fracking is something of a leap in the dark • 'exploitation' (although in this context can be entirely neutral) might suggest something undesirable, taking improper advantage of a situation • 'cost' suggests there will be adverse effects • 'U-turn' suggests backward-looking, almost cowardly

				• positioning of 'U-turn' as last word in the sentence emphasises writer's belief that this would be a retrograde step **Both:** • the structure of the final sentence carefully balances her views on the two sides around the semi-colon – the 'dream' contrasted with the 'plunge'; the point is underlined by the insertion of 'by contrast'. or any other acceptable answer.
7.		'Scotland stands … at a frightening crossroads' (lines 65–66). Evaluate the effectiveness of this metaphor as a way of describing the dilemma the Scottish Government faces about fracking. Candidates should discuss how effective they find the metaphor as a way of describing what the writer is saying in the passage as a whole. Marks will depend on the quality of comment. For full marks there must be reference to the metaphor and to the ideas of the passage as a whole. 2 marks may be awarded for detailed/insightful comment; 1 mark for a more basic comment; 0 marks for reference alone. *Possible answers are shown in the 'Additional guidance' column.*	3	Possible answers include: • the metaphor 'at a crossroads' suggests a choice of directions • throughout the passage she has argued that we have a choice between taking on board the economic benefits of fracking, despite the environmental dangers … • … and committing to renewable sources because of their environmental, greener credentials • it could quite profitably be argued that the metaphor is in fact a pretty sloppy, clichéd one, and/or that a 'crossroads' offers more than two options • reference could be made to the use earlier of 'U-turn' as an effective (or otherwise) preparation for another travel metaphor or any other acceptable answer.

Supplementary question

Imagine that in the exam the second passage is one that proclaims the virtues of renewable energy sources. The comparison question asks you to identify key areas on which the writers agree. Which two key ideas would you identify from this first passage?

Answer

- The number of resources Scotland has available to create renewable energy is large.
- That Scotland has the ability to sustain itself into the long term is an attractive prospect.
  (Remember that you are asked to produce evidence backing up these ideas.)

Commentary on supplementary question

You can eliminate the first two paragraphs – they are historical background.

The main section of the writer's argument dealing with fracking runs from lines 21 to 51, so you can skip that too.

The last paragraph is a balancing conclusion.

You are left therefore with paragraph 3 and paragraph 7 which are actually about the advantages of renewable energy in Scotland.

You have already, in answers to questions 2 and 6(a), dealt with these advantages, but here you have been asked, not for detail, but for 'key' ideas, so you have to generalise, either by combining ideas or by choosing the most important.

PASSAGE B – GAP YEARS

MARKING INSTRUCTIONS FOR EACH QUESTION

Question		Expected response	Max mark	Additional guidance
1.		**Identify in your own words two criticisms made of gap years in lines 1–14.** Candidates should identify two criticisms made of gap years. Candidates must use their own words. No marks are awarded for verbatim quotations from the passage. *1 mark for each point from the 'Additional guidance' column.*	2	Possible answers include: • those on gap years are not really cutting ties with home • those on gap years learn little or nothing about the country they are in • the idea that they are living without parental support is a sham or any other acceptable answer.
2.	a)	**Re-read lines 15–31. Explain in your own words why the writer thinks that the students on the train illustrate the unsatisfactory nature of gap years.** Candidates should explain why the writer thinks that the students on the train illustrate the unsatisfactory nature of gap years. Candidates must use their own words. No marks are awarded for verbatim quotations from the passage. *1 mark for each point from the 'Additional guidance' column.*	3	Possible answers include: • they were using their experiences as a way to seem better than others • alcohol consumption was their main topic • they displayed ignorance of the places to which they had been • they had spent their time with others on gap years and had not engaged with the local community • their gap year had just been an enjoyable diversion or any other acceptable answer.
2.	b)	**Re-read lines 15–31. Analyse how the writer's use of language in these lines makes fun of the students. In your answer you should refer to such features as word choice, sentence structure and tone.** Candidates should analyse how the writer's use of language makes fun of the students. Marks will depend on the quality of comment. For full marks there must be comment on at least two features. 2 marks may be awarded for reference plus detailed/insightful comment; 1 mark for reference plus more basic comment; 0 marks for reference alone. Thus 4 marks could be gained as 2 + 2 or 2 + 1 + 1 or 1 + 1 + 1 + 1. *Possible answers are shown in the 'Additional guidance' column.*	4	Possible answers include: • 'exquisite (for the listener) game' – the parenthesis shows that the students were unwittingly entertaining those on the train • 'one-upmanship' suggests they were showing off • 'God-I'm-sooooo-cool-I-can-hardly-speak' mocks their way of speaking by exaggerating their affected tone of voice • '– not that it mattered –' shows their lack of concern for where they had been, shows the gap year had taught them nothing • repetition of '(un-named)' emphasises their ignorance, lack of interest in where they had been

Answers for questions in Part Two

				• 'really soooo sweet' suggests patronising attitude towards the local people • 'gappie'/'gappies' – creation of diminutive term makes them sound childish • 'a jolly way to kill time' suggests the whole experience is trivial, self-indulgent • 'arrogance' suggests self-importance, overconfidence or any other acceptable answer.
3.	a)	**Re-read lines 32–41. Explain in your own words the key criticisms made of 'organised placements'.** Candidates should explain the key criticisms made of 'organised placements'. Candidates must use their own words. No marks are awarded for verbatim quotations from the passage. *1 mark for each point from the 'Additional guidance' column.*	2	Possible answers include: • they do not provide real opportunities for students to develop life skills • they do not allow/encourage students to make decisions for themselves • they are risk-free or any other acceptable answer.
3.	b)	**Re-read lines 32–41. Analyse how the writer's word choice and sentence structure in these lines make clear her negative view of 'organised placements'.** Candidates should analyse how the writer's word choice and sentence structure make clear her negative view of 'organised placements'. Marks will depend on the quality of comment. For full marks there must be comment on both features. 2 marks may be awarded for reference plus detailed/insightful comment; 1 mark for reference plus more basic comment; 0 marks for reference alone. Thus 4 marks could be gained as 2 + 2 or 2 + 1 + 1 or 1 + 1 + 1 + 1. *Possible answers are shown in the 'Additional guidance' column.*	4	Possible answers include: **Word choice:** • 'claimed' suggests it is not proven, only an assertion • 'some group leader' reduces the significance of the leader, as if they are all the same • 'pre-packaged' suggests all the hard work is done by someone else • 'specially made' suggests it is artificial, not real • 'playing at being a teacher' suggests it is not real, just for own enjoyment • 'all arranged' makes it clear that the students themselves have no part in the planning **Sentence structure:** • 'but' indicates that a negation will follow of the claim about being 'more productive' • repetition of 'or' suggests the extent of what these placements fail to achieve • periodic structure of final sentence: two 'if' clauses followed by minor concessions ('had a wonderful time … may even have learned'), then punches home with 'hardly the stuff of which heroes are made' or any other acceptable answer.

Answers for questions in Part Two

4.		**Using your own words, identify from lines 42–54 three possible advantages of a gap year.** Candidates should identify three possible advantages of a gap year. Candidates must use their own words. No marks are awarded for verbatim quotations from the passage. *1 mark for each point from the 'Additional guidance' column.*	3	Possible answers include: • participants gain some sense of living without constant supervision and protection • participants learn something about living independently • participants learn about how to be accountable for their actions • participants learn about how to get on with others in a group or any other acceptable answer.
5.	a)	**Re-read lines 55–69. Using your own words, identify three reasons the writer gives for suggesting that a gap year would be good for many Scottish young people.** Candidates should identify three reasons the writer gives for suggesting that a gap year would be good for many Scottish young people. Candidates must use their own words. No marks are awarded for verbatim quotations from the passage. *1 mark for each point from the 'Additional guidance' column.*	3	Possible answers include: • it would expand the very limited life experiences of many Scottish school-leavers • it would eliminate/reduce their dependence on home • it would shake them out of their complacency • it would improve their experience of university • it might lead some to realise that they are not suited to university (and thus reduce numbers leaving university without finishing) or any other acceptable answer.
5.	b)	**Re-read lines 55–69. By referring to at least two features of language in these lines, analyse how the writer emphasises the points she is making about Scottish school leavers.** Candidates should analyse how the writer emphasises the points she is making about Scottish school leavers. Marks will depend on the quality of comment. For full marks there must be comment on at least two features. 2 marks may be awarded for reference plus detailed/insightful comment; 1 mark for reference plus more basic comment; 0 marks for reference alone. Thus 4 marks could be gained as 2 + 2 or 2 + 1 + 1 or 1 + 1 + 1 + 1. *Possible answers are shown in the 'Additional guidance' column.*	4	Possible answers include: **Word choice:** • 'simply swapping' suggests going to university involves no great change in lifestyle or outlook • 'grim' suggests their situation is very bleak, depressing • 'parochialism' emphasises the narrow-mindedness of their outlook • 'shock therapy' suggests she thinks Scottish young people need to be forcibly shaken out of their safe, protected lives • 'shovelled (into the university system)' suggests school-leavers are being forced *en masse* into something without much thought • 'statistical cannon-fodder' suggests they are like soldiers being sent callously into battle, just numbers on a page, not valued individuals **Sentence structure:** • 'University should be a faintly alarming experience' – the short, simple sentence highlights the rather provocative nature of her view on what university should be like • the parenthetical 'however pre-packaged' acknowledges that many gap years are far from ideal

			Tone: • 'scarcely been beyond the end of the road' – exaggeration to emphasise how limited their experience of life is • 'being looked after by their mothers' – mockery of their lack of independence • 'leaped out of a plane without a parachute' – exaggerated, humorous way to describe her notion that young people at that age need to take risks, escape the comforts of home
			or any other acceptable answer.

Supplementary question

Imagine that in the exam the second passage is one in which the writer puts forward many positive points about gap years. The comparison question asks you to identify key areas on which the writers disagree. Which two key ideas would you identify from this first passage?

Answer

- The pretence of independence.
- The lack of any real knowledge gained from the experience.

(Remember that you are asked to produce evidence backing up these ideas.)

Commentary on supplementary question

Paragraphs 1 and 2 deal mainly with the lack of independence.

Lines 15–25 simply give an anecdote that exemplifies what the writer is talking about.

Paragraph 5 deals with the lack of knowledge that is gained from the experience.

Paragraph 6 repeats the idea that independence is not increased by gap years.

The remainder of the passage is about some advantages of a gap year, so it is not a 'disagreement'.

PASSAGE C – TATTOOS

MARKING INSTRUCTIONS FOR EACH QUESTION

Question		Expected response	Max mark	Additional guidance
1.	a)	**Re-read lines 1–31. Identify in your own words the key differences the writer sees between the people who had tattoos 20 years ago and those who have them now.** Candidates should identify the key differences the writer sees between the people who had tattoos 20 years ago and those who have them now. Candidates must use their own words. No marks are awarded for verbatim quotations from the passage. *1 mark for each point from the 'Additional guidance' column. For full marks both '20 years ago' and 'now' should be covered, but not necessarily in equal measure.*	4	Possible answers include: **Twenty years ago:** • worn by the lower/working/underclass • worn by those with low intelligence • associated with criminality • worn by low/non-achievers **Now:** • associated with sophistication • worn by wealthy people • worn by the social elite/high achievers • worn by educated people or any other acceptable answer.
1.	b)	**Re-read lines 1–31. By referring to at least two features, analyse how the writer uses language to convey his dislike for tattoos and/or the people who have them. You may wish to refer to such features as word choice, sentence structure and tone.** Candidates should analyse how the writer's use of language conveys his dislike for tattoos and the people who have them. Marks will depend on the quality of comment on appropriate language feature(s). For full marks there must be comment on at least two features. 2 marks may be awarded for reference plus detailed/insightful comment; 1 mark for reference plus more basic comment; 0 marks for reference alone. Thus 4 marks could be gained as 2 + 2 or 2 + 1 + 1 or 1 + 1 + 1 + 1. *Possible answers are shown in the 'Additional guidance' column.*	4	Possible answers include: **Word choice:** • 'pea brain' – insulting, suggests little/low intelligence • 'stain themselves' suggests tattooing is ugly, leaves blemishes • 'repulsive' suggests tattoos are hideous, foul, nauseating • 'sub-moronic smears' suggests they are just smudges or blotches • 'some mug' suggests the tattooist is nothing special • 'inky atrocities' suggests they are outrages, crimes against decency **Sentence structure:** • list ('pea brain … Sailor Man') – shows how many categories there are for him to despise • question ('Who…') – simply a device to allow him a sneering response • parenthesis ('first class …') allows emphasis on just how wealthy they are • 'the great and the good, the rich and famous' – as if reeling off a predictable list of all the types who now sport tattoos

Answers for questions in Part Two

				• sequence of short sentences ('Tattoos got …') sounds like a bored listing of all the ways tattoos have been accepted into mainstream society • single sentence paragraph ('Only one thing …') emphasises the simplicity of what he is saying, the rejection of the previous claims for sophistication; structured with a colon to introduce the harsh condemnation • questions ('What happened …') suggest incredulity and/or desire to explain, investigate **Tone:** • 'bunch of fat thickos and their ropey birds' – concentration of slang/colloquial words shows utter contempt • 'peeking from a fluffy robe' suggests cossetted, indulgent, showy • 'all these beautiful people' – clichéd phrase suggests a group of people who expect to be thought of this way • use of clichés such as 'cool', 'sexy', 'went mainstream' suggests a distaste for the justifications offered (and the 'got … got … went … got' suggests an element of laziness, sloppiness in the thinking/expression) • 'staining themselves with poorly drawn cartoons' – contemptuous description of tattoos, not as 'art' but as low-level drawings • 'up to their armpits' shows distaste by referring to a less than romantic part of the body • inverted commas at 'body art' suggests it is not a term with which he agrees or any other acceptable answer.
2.		**'Now tattoos attempt to represent the antithesis of tribal identity' (line 44). By referring in detail to lines 32–47, explain how the writer develops this idea.** Candidates should explain what the writer means by 'Now tattoos attempt to represent the antithesis of tribal identity'. Candidates must use their own words. No marks are awarded for verbatim quotations from the passage. *1 mark for each point from the 'Additional guidance' column.*	4	Possible answers include: • in the distant past tattoos marked out the race or community to which you belonged • in the recent past they did the same for a social class or work grouping • now it's the opposite • instead of marking people out as distinct … • … they make everyone look the same or any other acceptable answer.

Answers for questions in Part Two

3.		**Identify the writer's tone in lines 48–51 and analyse how it is conveyed.** Candidates should identify the writer's tone and analyse how it is conveyed. Marks will depend on the identification of a suitable tone and on quality of comment. 1 mark for identifying a suitable tone, then: 2 marks may be awarded for detailed/insightful comment; 1 mark for more basic comment; 0 marks for no comment. *Possible answers are shown in the 'Additional guidance' column.*	3	Possible answers include: **Tone:** • dismissive, sneering, contemptuous, condescending, etc. **Comment:** • 'lager vomit' suggests over-indulgence, lack of self-respect • 'dribbling' suggests slavering, baby-like, lack of control • 'white shell suit' suggests the ultimate in bad dress sense • 'dopey' suggests they are childishly stupid • the alliteration in 'dopey little dolphins done' makes it sound childlike • 'empty lives' suggests how insubstantial he thinks they are • 'lukewarm' – ironic wordplay on 'cool' • 'ancient' suggests hopeless, past it, out of touch or any other acceptable answer.
4.		**By referring to lines 52–60, explain in your own words why the writer thinks his father's tattoos were acceptable.** Candidates should explain why the writer thinks his father's tattoos were acceptable. Candidates must use their own words. No marks are awarded for verbatim quotations from the passage. *1 mark for each point from the 'Additional guidance' column.*	3	Possible answers include: • because they were signs of his manliness, virility • because they were part of his life in the navy • because what they depicted (knife and wife's name) were simple, personal, reasonable, understandable • because they contained nothing that made him feel uneasy • because it was at a time when tattoos were unremarkable for the kind of person the father was or any other acceptable answer.
5.		**Identify in your own words three key points the writer makes about tattoos in lines 61–71.** Candidates should identify three key points the writer makes about tattoos. Candidates must use their own words. No marks are awarded for verbatim quotations from the passage. *1 mark for each point from the 'Additional guidance' column.*	3	Possible answers include: • they don't make anything or anyone better than they originally are • they don't add beauty or desirability • their use by celebrities has encouraged 'ordinary' people to get them • they can actually detract from natural good looks • they seem to encourage their wearers to think they are clever, sophisticated or any other acceptable answer.

Answers for questions in Part Two

6.	**Evaluate the effectiveness of the final paragraph (lines 72–74) as a conclusion to the passage as a whole. You should refer in your answer to ideas and tone.**	4	Possible answers include:
	Candidates should evaluate the effectiveness of the final paragraph as a conclusion to the passage as a whole.		• the offhand, dismissive term 'painted people', as if they were one amorphous group, is in keeping with the tone used throughout the passage to describe and depersonalise people with tattoos
	Marks will depend on the evaluation of the effectiveness of the final paragraph and on the quality of comment on ideas and tone.		• 'react with wild indignation' – depicts those with tattoos as being easily offended, unaware that there might be anything wrong – all in keeping with his presentation of them as self-centred, stupid, unaware of how they look
	2 marks may be awarded for a detailed/insightful comment; 1 mark for more basic comment; 0 marks for reference alone. Thus 4 marks could be gained as 2 + 2 or 2 + 1 + 1 or 1 + 1 + 1 + 1.		• 'cock a dismayed eyebrow' – a rather roundabout, perhaps deliberately understated, way of expressing disapproval, perhaps emphasising how touchy they are
	Possible answers are shown in the 'Additional guidance' column.		• structure/balance of the final sentence ('not the victims … just the victims') – a rather elegant dismissal of a serious objection ('prejudice') with a typically reductive description of the tattooist as 'someone who can't draw very well' (cf the earlier 'some mug with an O Level in art')
			or any other acceptable answer.

Answers for questions in Part Three – Section 1

EXERCISE 1 – DOES MAN FLU REALLY EXIST?

Identify two key areas on which the writers disagree. In your answer, you should refer in detail to both passages.

Sample answer 1 (bullet points)

- 'Yes' says that 'man flu' is real and should be taken seriously – 'man flu is real' – and uses the results of the Cambridge research to back up his statement.

  'No' says that 'man flu' is made up and doesn't exist – 'Man flu is a clever ploy' – and says that she doesn't believe the research because it was done by a man.

- 'Yes' says that a man's partner should tend to his needs – 'If you hear a bell ringing, girls, stick the kettle on' – because he is really ill and needs his symptoms to be treated.

  'No' says that women should leave men alone and not spoil them – 'Let them sniff and get on with it' – because if she ignores him he will have to get up sooner rather than later.

Sample answer 2 (continuous prose)

The writer of the first extract (writer A) believes that the research vindicates men's correctness in thinking that they are badly affected by infections. He gives the researcher his title, 'Dr', and mentions 'Cambridge University' to back up his opinion that the research is respectable and true.

Writer B scoffs at the results of the research: 'Was this study led by a man, perchance?', suggesting that the researcher was biased in favour of men's point of view because of his gender, and that 'man flu' is more likely to be a 'malingering gene' than a weakened immune system.

Writer A says that now the research has proved that the illness is real, men need to be treated to a great deal of help and support – 'sympathy, soup … stick the kettle on'.

Writer B thinks that, as the illness is not real, or is at least exaggerated, there is no need to pander to a man's comfort, because if attention is not showered on him he will get up quicker – 'Let them sniff and get on with it.'

Commentary

Both sample answers 1 and 2 have identified correctly the two areas of disagreement.

The writer of answer 1 has provided back-up for her identification by quoting from the passages and linking the quotations to the writer's opinion.

The writer of answer 2 gives a fuller description of the main areas of disagreement (without, however, going into unnecessary detail) and provides evidence, in the form of explanation and quotation, to back up her identification of the main areas.

EXERCISE 2 – CCTV IN SCHOOLS

Identify key areas on which the writers disagree. In your answer you should refer in detail to both passages.

The writers disagree in the following ways:

- Passage 1 says cameras don't cut crime – 'Does it really reduce bullying', and '[they are] at best ineffective, at worst negative' – are given as evidence for this.

    In contrast, passage 2 says cameras do cut crime, and gives as evidence the fact that there have been almost no incidents since the cameras were installed.

- Passage 1 says that cameras used for surveillance are an intrusion – 'sensitivity of recording young people' is seen as a bad thing.

    Passage 2 says that the cameras are for safeguarding, not surveillance – 'tapes are only viewed by one person and only if an incident takes place'.

- Passage 1 says that parents may object to their child being recorded: 'feel the camera is intrusive'.

    Passage 2 says that parents like the cameras because they keep pupils safe – the 'nods of approval' that parents give when they hear about the safety angle.

- Passage 1 says the regulations governing the use of cameras are too weak; there are no powers of enforcement, so there is no real control.

    Passage 2 says the regulations have governed what they have done, and the number of their cameras, suggesting that the rules have been followed.

Commentary

You probably found that when you made rough notes on passage 2, you ended up with four points, one from each paragraph:

- cameras are for safeguarding
- they are not surveillance – they reduce crime
- the cameras comply with the regulations
- parents like them

This gives you four areas of disagreement. You have to decide whether each of these is a key area. In this case four is probably the correct number.

EXERCISE 3 – JFK

Identify key areas on which the writers agree about JFK. In your answer you should refer in detail to both passages.

- His charisma/ability to inspire:

    passage 1 – his personal appearance was attractive and dynamic

    passage 2 – his feel for the importance of inspirational leadership – vital at the centre of government

- His ability as a communicator – especially on TV:

    passage 1 – he understood and exploited TV, using it to create his celebrity status and legend

    passage 2 – he relied on the spoken word, and TV ensured that millions heard and saw him

- His idealistic legacy:

  passage 1 talks about the formation of the Peace Corps, and the vision of the Moon landings

  passage 2 talks about founding the Peace Corps and his call for Moon missions

- He had faults but they can be overlooked in the face of his achievements:

  passage 1 says that much of the myth was fake

  passage 2 talks about a 'litany of complaints' and 'critics scoff at his image'

  (A possible area of agreement is the idea of his assassination creating the longevity of his memory, but that is perhaps not really a 'key area'.)

Commentary

This answer is written as a series of bullet points. You could also write the same points in continuous prose. The first point might look like this:

'A key area of agreement is Kennedy's attractiveness and his inspirational qualities – he appeared young and dynamic, unlike previous presidents, and became an example to aspire to (passage 1). Passage 2 says he realised the importance of the president being inspirational and encouraging, and used his personal attractiveness to influence people – moving the country on.'

The advantage of writing in continuous prose is that it is easier to link your thoughts together to explain the agreement.

You should practise both methods and see which one suits you best.

Answers for questions in Part Three – Section 2

It is not recommended that students' efforts at this stage be formally assessed or be awarded a mark out of 5.

EXERCISE 4 – THE FIRST WORLD WAR

Both writers express their views about the commemoration of the outbreak of the First World War. Identify key areas on which they agree.

The table below outlines some of the points that could have been made under the headings given, although other points (and possibly other areas) could be identified.

	Area of agreement	Simon Jenkins	Grace Dent
1.	Coverage in the media	• excessive; distasteful/insensitive ('a media theme park'; 'BBC has gone mad')	• extensive; overdone ('another outside broadcast unit in another corner of the Commonwealth …')
2.	The real horrors of war	• undoubtedly 'terrible', but this applies to all wars	• 'killed millions …'; 'futile massacre'; 'unspeakable pointless carnage'
3.	Writer's attitude to the commemorations	• inappropriate; 'banal … pornography of violence'; seem to be celebrating victory, not commemorating the dead	• inappropriate: dominated by royalty; politicians being consciously 'sombre'; refers to a 'grand fuss'; 'mere cliché'
4.	Have lessons been learned?	• no – despite all the sanctimonious statements, we have in the past ten years been at war (unnecessarily) three times; lessons, if ever learned, 'are then forgotten'	• no – wars still being fought in many places; 'not one iota … had been learned'

EXERCISE 5 – SERVING ON A JURY

Both writers express their views about serving on a jury. Identify key areas on which they disagree.

(**Point of interest:** The headlines given to the published articles were 'The depressing reality of jury service' and 'Serving on a jury restored my faith in humanity'.)

First: Identify very briefly the key difference of opinion about the jury system.

- Lewin thinks it is poor, inefficient, unsatisfactory …
- Steel thinks it works well, is admirable …

Now: To help you identify further points of disagreement, draw up a table similar to the one below and complete it with appropriate details.

The version below is offered as a possible approach to this question. Note that while all the 'evidence' here is given in the form of quotation, this is largely a by-product of the tabular format and it should be remembered that evidence can come in other forms. If quotation is used, it should be kept as brief as possible.

	Matthew Lewin		Mark Steel	
	Opinion	Evidence	Opinion	Evidence
The experience of serving on a jury	it was disheartening, discouraging	'faith … severely battered'	it was uplifting, inspiring	'exhilarating'
Their fellow jurors in general	very critical	'deeply ignorant people'	likes, admires them	'inspiring enthusiasm'
Social spread of fellow jurors	narrow	'shortage of the middle classes'	wide	'advertising executive', 'nurse', '[someone who looked like a] headmistress'
Attitude to the accused	sees them as probably guilty	'obviously guilty criminals'; 'no matter how damning the evidence'	sympathetic	'timid'; 'I felt bad for'; 'lad'

Then: Add one (or more than one) more point to the left-hand column and fill in the relevant details.

The following points could be made:

	Matthew Lewin		Mark Steel	
	Opinion	Evidence	Opinion	Evidence
Jurors' ability to follow process	very limited	'no analytical ability'	satisfactory	all of lines 29–36; 'methodically'
Jurors' note-taking	uneven	'many … neglected to take notes'	thorough	'Everyone had taken notes'
Jurors' attitude to accused	keen to believe innocent	'a mission to acquit'	open-minded	'had taken their responsibility incredibly seriously'

Finally: In terms of constructing a full exam-style response, the primary concern will be to establish which are the 'key' areas. A possible answer is:

- the overall effectiveness of the jury system
- the degree to which serving on a jury is a rewarding experience
- the abilities of fellow jurors
- the attitudes of fellow jurors

Answers for questions in Part Three – Section 2

EXERCISE 6 – COMPETITIVE SPORT

Both writers express their views about competitive sport for young people. Identify key areas on which they agree.

First: Identify very briefly the key point of similarity in the writers' attitudes to competitive sport for young people.

- They both believe that competitive sport is good for young people, that valuable lessons can be learned from losing, that it is character-building, and so on.

Next: Work through each passage, answering the questions below in note form.

Passage 1

1. **Very briefly, describe the writer's feelings about 'school sports days' in:**
    a) **lines 1–7.**
       fond memories, nostalgic, slightly amused
    b) **lines 8–13.**
       genuine admiration, appreciation
    c) **lines 14–20.**
       admits some negatives, but insists they were 'fun'

2. **Re-read lines 22–26.**
    a) **Why, according to the writer, has the 'zone sport day' been introduced in a number of schools?**
       because many schools disapprove of the competitive nature of the traditional type of sports day
    b) **What is the writer's attitude to the 'zone sport day'?**
       she is critical, dismissive, scathing, contemptuous

3. **Re-read lines 27–46.**
    a) **What impression does the writer create in lines 32–35 of the 'zone sport day'?**
       that it does not engage the children's interest
    b) **Explain the difference of opinion, in lines 36–39, between the writer and the advocates of the 'zone sport day'.**
       advocates believe it means children are not spending time just standing watching others; the writer believes there are lessons to be learned from watching others
    c) **What is the writer's main criticism in lines 40–46 of the 'zone sport day'?**
       it is meaningless/futile for the children; the children don't understand what it is all about (**NB:** not 'it is boring to watch', which is not her main criticism: 'More than tedious, it is depressing to watch the children …')

4. **What reasons does the writer give in the final paragraph (lines 47–54) in favour of the return of the traditional sports day?**
    - competition is a good thing
    - it sharpens the way people think
    - it teaches people to lose with dignity

Passage 2

5. **What key point is the writer making in lines 1–12?**
   defeat at football/sport can cause deep emotional harm

6. **What, according to the writer, are the changes she describes in lines 13–17 designed to achieve?**
   to reduce/minimise the (alleged) suffering caused to children by defeat

7. **What point does the anecdote in lines 18–22 add to the writer's argument?**
   it reinforces the idea of bureaucratic interference to 'protect' children

8. **From lines 23–35, identify the key points the writer makes to justify her opinion that the 'well-meaning officials' (line 23) are wrong.**
   Several points are made, but the following are probably the 'key' ones:
   - learning how to accept defeat is an important process for children
   - children will think there is no need to strive to do their best
   - children have an innate desire to out-do their peers

9. **According to the writer in lines 36–44, what important benefits do children derive from sport?**
   Several points are made, but the following are probably the 'important' ones:
   - it encourages teamwork and a sense of community
   - it allows a platform for rivalry and hostility to be enacted in safe and organised conditions
   - learning how to lose enhances the joy of winning

Areas of agreement

Both writers express their views about competitive sport for young people. Identify key areas on which they agree. In your answer, you should refer in detail to both passages.

You may answer this question in continuous prose or in a series of developed bullet points.

The key areas of agreement are:
- competitive sport is good for young people
- it teaches important lessons about life, especially how to lose
- claims that it can damage young people psychologically are overstated
- alternatives to competitive sport are all unsatisfactory
- the alternatives are devised/promoted by people who don't understand the value of competitive sport

Answers for questions in Part Three – Section 3

EXERCISE 7 – TEENAGERS

Both writers express their views about teenagers. Identify key areas on which they disagree. In your answer, you should refer in detail to both passages.

You may answer this question in continuous prose or in a series of developed bullet points.

Expected response	Max mark	Additional guidance
Candidates should identify key areas of disagreement in the two passages. There may be some overlap among the areas of agreement. Markers will have to judge the extent to which a candidate has covered two points or one. Candidates can use bullet points in this question, or write a number of linked statements. Evidence from the passage may include quotations, but these should be supported by explanations. *Approach to marking is shown in the 'Additional guidance' column.* *Key areas of disagreement are shown in the grid below. Other answers are possible.*	5	The mark for this question should reflect the quality of response in two areas: • identification of the key areas of disagreement in attitude/ideas • level of detail given in support The following guidelines should be used: • **5 marks** – identification of three key areas of disagreement with insightful use of supporting evidence • **4 marks** – identification of three key areas of disagreement with appropriate use of supporting evidence • **3 marks** – identification of three key areas of disagreement • **2 marks** – identification of two key areas of disagreement • **1 mark** – identification of one key area of disagreement • **0 marks** – failure to identify one key area of disagreement and/or misunderstanding of task

	Area of disagreement	Jenny McCartney	Kate Figgis
1.	General attitude	• admits fear of teenagers	• proclaims her love of them
2.	Response to their behaviour	• sees them as rowdy	• sees them as fun
3.	Role of adults/adult authority	• calls for a resurgence of adult authority	• wants teenagers to stand up to/challenge adult authority
4.	Attitude to youth culture	• sees youth culture as intimidating	• sees youth culture as something to be admired
5.	Teenagers' concern for others	• teenagers don't understand/care about how others think	• teenagers are deeply concerned about others' wellbeing

Answers for questions in Part Three – Section 3

EXERCISE 8 – THE IMPORTANCE OF READING

Both writers express their views about the importance of reading among children. Identify key areas on which they agree and on which they disagree. In your answer, you should refer in detail to both passages.

You may answer this question in continuous prose or in a series of developed bullet points.

Expected response	Max mark	Additional guidance
Candidates should identify key areas of agreement and disagreement in the two passages. There may be some overlap among the areas of agreement. Markers will have to judge the extent to which a candidate has covered two points or one. Candidates can use bullet points in this question, or write a number of linked statements. Evidence from the passage may include quotations, but these should be supported by explanations. *Approach to marking is shown in the 'Additional guidance' column.* *Key areas of agreement and disagreement are shown in the grids below. Other answers are possible.*	5	The mark for this question should reflect the quality of response in two areas: • identification of the key areas of agreement and disagreement in attitude/ideas • level of detail given in support To score 2 or more marks, there must be at least one area of agreement and one area of disagreement given. The following guidelines should be used: • **5 marks** – comprehensive identification of three or more key areas of agreement and disagreement with full use of supporting evidence • **4 marks** – clear identification of three or more key areas of agreement and disagreement with relevant use of supporting evidence • **3 marks** – identification of three or more key areas of agreement and disagreement with supporting evidence • **2 marks** – identification of two key areas of agreement and disagreement with supporting evidence • **1 mark** – identification of one key area of agreement or disagreement with supporting evidence • **0 marks** – failure to identify any key area of agreement or disagreement and/or total misunderstanding of task

	Area of agreement	Michael Morpurgo	Anthony Horowitz
1.	Reading is important/gives pleasure	• reading can change and enrich	• his love of books and reading ('can't imagine my life without it')
2.	Level of reading among children	• concern at numbers not reading; millions never become readers	• questions being asked; it's a 'hot topic'; big government initiative
3.	Quality/quantity of books being published	• 10,000 children's books per annum; 'publishers who publish too much rubbish'	• criticisms of Dan Brown, Jeffrey Archer, Mills & Boon
4.	Adults/parents are not encouraging by example	• parents who don't read (to their children); teachers who use books inappropriately	• parents who make reading a sort of status symbol for their children; parents themselves perhaps not reading

Answers for questions in Part Three – Section 3

	Area of disagreement	Michael Morpurgo	Anthony Horowitz
5.	Benefits of reading	• reading is important in the development of the individual	• reading does not in itself make you a good person
6.	Schemes to encourage reading	• schemes (such as visits and readings) to encourage reading are commendable	• schemes (such as Booktrust/ the Government's) to encourage reading are questionable, potentially dangerous
7.	Promoting reading in general	• reading should be encouraged at every opportunity	• reading shouldn't be forced on anyone

EXERCISE 9 – SEX EDUCATION

Both writers express their views about sex education in schools. Identify key areas on which they agree and on which they disagree. In your answer, you should refer in detail to both passages.

You may answer this question in continuous prose or in a series of developed bullet points.

Expected response	Max mark	Additional guidance
Candidates should identify key areas of agreement and disagreement in the two passages. There may be some overlap among the areas of agreement. Markers will have to judge the extent to which a candidate has covered two points or one. Candidates can use bullet points in this question, or write a number of linked statements. Evidence from the passage may include quotations, but these should be supported by explanations. *Approach to marking is shown in the 'Additional guidance' column.* *Key areas of agreement and disagreement are shown in the grids below. Other answers are possible.*	5	The mark for this question should reflect the quality of response in two areas: • identification of the key areas of agreement and disagreement in attitude/ideas • level of detail given in support To score 2 or more marks, there must be at least one area of agreement and one area of disagreement. The following guidelines should be used: • **5 marks** – identification of three key areas of agreement and disagreement with insightful use of supporting evidence • **4 marks** – identification of three key areas of agreement and disagreement with appropriate use of supporting evidence • **3 marks** – identification of three key areas of agreement and disagreement • **2 marks** – identification of two key areas of agreement and disagreement • **1 mark** – identification of one key area of agreement or disagreement • **0 marks** – failure to identify one key area of agreement or disagreement and/or misunderstanding of task

Answers for questions in Part Three – Section 3

	Area of agreement	Joyce McMillan	Minette Marrin
1.	Is sex education working satisfactorily?	• no – many young people clearly not learning properly ('just can't seem to associate what they are told about sex at school with what happens in their own lives'; 'so many teenagers all at sea in this key area of their lives')	• no – extensive evidence/ statistics offered ('sex education has been an utter failure')
2.	Should sex education start young?	• yes – 'we all know that five-year-olds need to know a little bit about sex'	• yes – has no fundamental problem with the fpa booklet (aimed at 6-year-olds)
3.	Capable of arousing strong feelings	• media/public reaction can be extreme; 'shock-horror headlines'; 'the old atavistic monster rears up'	• her own rejection of more Government-inspired lessons ('What I really object to'; 'pervasive assumption'; 'That's nonsense'; 'The thought … is terrifying')

	Area of disagreement	Joyce McMillan	Minette Marrin
4.	Where the main responsibility lies	• school/society in general	• parents
5.	Causes of sexual promiscuity	• complex range of social problems ('a blizzard of social reasons')	• too much sex education ('tempted to argue that sex education causes sexual delinquency')
6.	The solution/way forward	• no simple solution offered ('move forward as a whole society, rather than as a bunch of fragmented individuals')	• leave it to the parents; keep teachers and Government out of it

Marking guidelines for Part Four

These marking guidelines have been written to replicate the style of Marking Instructions used by SQA. This should help teachers/lecturers advise their students about the best way to answer and how marks will be allocated.

These detailed instructions can, and should, however, be used for more than simply marking students' responses – the additional points (especially in the questions calling for analysis) should be seen as a useful teaching tool. Exploring *all* the possible answers on word choice, sentence structure, and so on, is a very worthwhile classroom exercise for teachers and students alike.

NB: For ease of reference, the exact wording of each question is given, in bold, at the start of the relevant 'Expected response' column. This differs from SQA practice.

Answers to questions on imagery: Please note that the 'Just as … so …' approach used here is a suggestion only and is **not** required by SQA, who do not ask that candidates identify the literal root of an image before progressing to analysing it. However, it is an approach that the authors feel is helpful to both students and teachers as a way to learn about analysing imagery.

PAPER 1 – HOMEWORK

MARKING INSTRUCTIONS FOR EACH QUESTION

Question		Expected response	Max mark	Additional guidance
1.		**By referring to lines 1–10, explain in your own words why the writer agrees so strongly with the poem 'Toads'.** Candidates should explain in their own words why the writer agrees so strongly with the poem 'Toads'. Candidates must use their own words. No marks are awarded for verbatim quotations from the passage. *1 mark for each point from the 'Additional guidance' column.*	3	Possible answers include: • he agrees with Larkin that work is an unpleasant, disagreeable influence in life (explanation of 'squat') • because work has inhibited his behaviour in many ways (explanation of 'controlled'/'constrained') • he feels that work has influenced his life (explanation of 'coloured') • he feels that work has controlled/dominated his life (explanation of 'bowing to it') or any other acceptable answer.
2.	a)	**Re-read lines 11–21. Identify two key problems the writer suffered as a result of working hard at school.** Candidates should identify two key problems the writer suffered as a result of working hard at school.	2	Possible answers include: • he had no time to enjoy himself/relax (explanation of 'social life was the opposite [of sparkling]') • his life was focused exclusively on schoolwork (explanation of 'As for any interest in the world outside')

Marking guidelines for Part Four

		Candidates must use their own words. No marks are awarded for verbatim quotations from the passage. *1 mark for each point from the 'Additional guidance' column.*		• this left him with a sense that he was doing something wrong any time he wasn't working (explanation of 'guilt … persisted into university and adult life') or any other acceptable answer.
2.	b)	**Re-read lines 11–21. By referring to at least two features of language in these lines, analyse how the writer's use of language conveys the unpleasantness he associates with schoolwork. In your answer you should refer to features such as word choice, sentence structure, imagery …** Candidates should analyse how the writer's use of language conveys the unpleasantness he associates with schoolwork. Marks will depend on the quality of comment on appropriate language feature(s). For full marks there must be comment on at least two features. 2 marks may be awarded for reference plus detailed/insightful comment; 1 mark for reference plus more basic comment; 0 marks for reference alone. Thus 4 marks could be gained as 2 + 2 or 2 + 1 + 1 or 1 + 1 + 1 + 1. *Possible answers are shown in the 'Additional guidance' column.*	4	Possible answers include: **Word choice:** • 'competing' suggests it was all about being better than someone or something else • 'fiercely' suggests it was aggressive, brutal • 'slog' suggests laborious, unpleasant, unrewarding • 'nagging' suggests something that lingers, can't be got rid of **Sentence structure:** • dash introduces an expansion of 'slog' that emphasises the relentless nature of the work • repetition – 'hours and hours' gives the impression of endless amounts of time • list-like structure of 'hours and hours of it, after school, every evening' suggests a gruelling, unremitting process • semicolon to balance 'At 14 …'/'By 17 …' highlights the inexorable progression • question ('…how could I') creates a despairing, defeated tone **Imagery:** • 'hung over me like a cloud' – just as a dark cloud contains a threat of imminent downpour, so his schoolwork was always in his mind, gloomy, menacing or any other acceptable answer.
3.		**Identify four negative effects of homework the writer gives in lines 22–36.** Candidates should identify four negative effects of homework the writer gives. Candidates must use their own words. No marks are awarded for verbatim quotations from the passage. *1 mark for each point from the 'Additional guidance' column.*	4	Possible answers include: • it becomes a form of emotional, psychological torture (explanation of 'mental oppression') • it turns a lot of people away from learning (explanation of 'alienates many') • it makes some people abnormally dedicated to work (explanation of 'cosmic conscientiousness') … • … such that it damages them for ever (explanation of 'blight the rest of their lives') • … and destroys their potential to benefit the community (explanation of 'could be so vital for society') • it prevents children from being exposed to other worthwhile activities/pastimes (explanation of 'giving children the time and opportunities to discover the infinite richness and possibilities of life') or any other acceptable answer.

Marking guidelines for Part Four

| 4. | | The writer's tone when he is describing the effects of school league tables in lines 37–41 is one of contempt. By referring closely to these lines, analyse how his use of language creates this tone. In your answer you should refer to such features as word choice, imagery, sentence structure … | 4 | Possible answers include:
Word choice
• 'fetish' suggests obsession, fixating, with a hint of something a little unwholesome
• 'forced' suggests pressure, compulsion, teachers are given no choice
• 'factories' suggests schools have become industrialised, dehumanised, merely churning out a product
• 'stacks of homework' suggests the homework is just a series of bundles, lacking in intellectual value
• 'blinkered' suggests the system is narrow-minded, inflexible
• 'grindingly utilitarian' suggests something relentlessly and damagingly driven by easily measurable, functional outcomes
Imagery
• 'fetish' – just as a fetish is, in primitive society, an object with magical powers, so league tables are looked on as all important in measuring the quality of education
• 'factories' – just as a factory carries out an industrial process to produce manufactured objects, so schools have become dehumanised, focused on measurable output
• 'blinkered' – just as blinkers are designed to narrow a horse's vision (to increase its chances of winning a race), so league tables are depriving students of a wider outlook on life by focusing on exam results only
Sentence structure
• the hyphenated structure of 'fact-cramming, rote-learning factories' suggests compression, pressure; imitates the repetitive sound of a relentless operation
• the repetitive structure of 'as blinkered, as grindingly utilitarian' suggests the relentless, grinding down nature of the process
• the rhetorical question 'Is it any wonder …?' suggests it's all too predictable
• the list of exaggerated details in 'shopping, watching telly and binge-drinking' sounds like a deliberate attempt to parody the standard criticisms of teenagers

or any other acceptable answer. |
| | | Candidates should analyse how the writer's use of language creates a contemptuous tone.

Marks will depend on the quality of comment on appropriate language features. For full marks there must be comment on at least two features.

2 marks may be awarded for reference plus detailed/insightful comment; 1 mark for reference plus more basic comment; 0 marks for reference alone.

Possible answers are shown in the 'Additional Guidance' column. | | |

Marking guidelines for Part Four

5.	**Re-read lines 42–53. Explain what advantages the writer thinks would come from a reduction in homework, but why it might be difficult to achieve.** Candidates should explain what advantages the writer thinks would come from a reduction in homework, but why it might be difficult to achieve. Candidates must use their own words. No marks are awarded for verbatim quotations from the passage. *1 mark for each point from the 'Additional guidance' column.*	4	Possible answers include: **Advantages:** • it would allow pupils to widen the scope of their studies (explanation of 'broader exploration of the world') • it would add to the fostering, cultivation of students as a whole (explanation of 'nurturing of a rounded individual') **Why difficult to achieve:** • because opportunities for various activities have been reduced recently (explanation of 'playing fields … after-school groups') • because parents like homework as it allows them to abdicate their own responsibilities (explanation of 'only too grateful … don't feel any obligation to devise activities themselves') • because teachers have become habituated to the limited, exam-focused approach to teaching (explanation of 'conditioned to following a narrow curriculum') or any other acceptable answer.
6.	**Evaluate the effectiveness of the last two paragraphs (lines 54–59) as a conclusion to the passage as a whole. You should refer in your answer to ideas and language.** Candidates should evaluate the effectiveness of the last two paragraphs as a conclusion to the passage as a whole. Marks will depend on the quality of comment on the effectiveness of the last two paragraphs. For full marks there must be comment on ideas and language. 2 marks may be awarded for detailed/insightful comment; 1 mark for more basic comment; 0 marks for reference alone. Thus 4 marks could be gained as 2 + 2 or 2 + 1 + 1 or 1 + 1 + 1 + 1. *Possible answers are shown in the 'Additional guidance' column.*	4	Possible answers include: • negative descriptions of homework ('piling … mountains … drudgery') are similar to the language and ideas elsewhere in the passage • negative descriptions of the effects of homework ('curiosity dies and a soulless, sullen, mechanistic compliance takes over') are similar to the language and ideas elsewhere in the passage • reference to Larkin picks up the opening of the passage, which began the idea of work as overpowering, restrictive • 'got them in his clutches for life' is a depressing, rather unsettling idea, reflecting the writer's admission near the start of the passage • the final paragraph is a brutally simple recognition of his own feelings or any other acceptable answer.

Marking guidelines for Part Four

| 7. | | **Both writers express their views about homework. Identify key areas on which they disagree.**

Candidates should identify key areas of disagreement in the two passages.

There may be some overlap among the areas of disagreement. Markers will have to judge the extent to which a candidate has covered two points or one.

Candidates can use bullet points in this final question, or write a number of linked statements.

Evidence from the passage may include quotations, but these should be supported by explanations.

Approach to marking is shown in the 'Additional guidance' column.

Key areas of disagreement are shown in the grid overleaf. Other answers are possible. | 5 | The mark for this question should reflect the quality of response in two areas:
• identification of the key areas of disagreement in attitude/ideas
• level of detail given in support

The following guidelines should be used:
• **5 marks** – identification of three key areas of disagreement with insightful use of supporting evidence
• **4 marks** – identification of three key areas of disagreement with appropriate use of supporting evidence
• **3 marks** – identification of three key areas of disagreement
• **2 marks** – identification of two key areas of disagreement
• **1 mark** – identification of one key area of disagreement
• **0 marks** – failure to identify one key area of disagreement and/or misunderstanding of task |

	Area of disagreement	**Richard Morrison**	**Eleanor Mills**
1.	General	• homework is a bad thing	• homework is a good thing
2.	Plans to reduce/abolish homework	• welcomes this enthusiastically	• thinks this is wrong/ misguided
3.	Educational benefits/short-term effects of homework	• none, more likely to cause students to switch off from education	• reinforces what's been taught at school that day
4.	Attitude to homework's effect on attainment	• (probably) leads to good grades, but at enormous social and psychological cost	• seems to imply that achieving good grades through homework is unquestionably a good thing
5.	Long-term effects	• disastrous – can make people damagingly obsessed with work	• is character-building; reinforces concept of 'deferred gratification'; shows that effort will be rewarded – an important lesson for life
6.	Effect on families	• encourages/allows parents to abdicate responsibility for inspiring children	• can create a sense of bonding between parent and child; can provide support, structure and purpose to disorganised families

PAPER 2 – *BREAKING BAD*

MARKING INSTRUCTIONS FOR EACH QUESTION

Question		Expected response	Max mark	Additional guidance
1.		**Analyse how the writer's word choice in lines 1–8 emphasises the change in Walter White in the course of the series.** Candidates should analyse how the writer's word choice emphasises the change in Walter White in the course of the series. Marks will depend on the quality of comment on word choice. For full marks there must be comment on 'before' and 'after'. 2 marks may be awarded for reference plus detailed/insightful comment; 1 mark for reference plus more basic comment; 0 marks for reference alone. Thus 4 marks could be gained as 2 + 2 or 2 + 1 + 1 or 1 + 1 + 1 + 1. *Possible answers are shown in the 'Additional guidance' column.*	4	Possible answers include: **Before:** • 'ordinary' depicts him as normal, typical, conventional, nothing special • 'dull' depicts him as boring, uninteresting • 'middle-aged' might be seen as suggesting conservative, settled • 'provide comfortably for his family' might be seen as suggesting mainstream, conventional aspiration **After:** • 'descended' suggests a decline, degeneration • 'sulphurous' suggests toxic, hellish, satanic • 'depths of evil' suggests extremes of wickedness • 'destroyed' suggests total demolition, devastation • 'ruthlessness' suggests cold-blooded, cruel or any other acceptable answer.
2.	a)	**Re-read lines 9–21. Identify in your own words what, according to the writer, makes *Breaking Bad* 'Dickensian'.** Candidates should identify in their own words what, according to the writer, makes *Breaking Bad* 'Dickensian'. Candidates must use their own words. No marks are awarded for verbatim quotations from the passage. *1 mark for each point from the 'Additional guidance' column.*	4	Possible answers include: • the characters are strong, compelling, realistic, credible (explanation of 'powerful, believable characters') • the setting is up to date, present day (explanation of 'contemporary') • the story follows characters' lives for an extended time (explanation of 'and allows their lives to play out over a long period of time') • there is an exploration of the way we live, a critique of contemporary mores (explanation of 'deconstruct our society') • it exploits the serial form to entice the audience (explanation of 'drip-fed his stories … hooked his public … hanging on his every word') • its producers are commercially savvy (reference to 'complete novel … box set') or any other acceptable answer.

Marking guidelines for Part Four

| 2. | b) | **Re-read lines 16–29. Analyse how the sentence structure in these lines clarifies what the writer is saying about *Breaking Bad*.**

Candidates should analyse how the sentence structure clarifies what the writer is saying about *Breaking Bad*.

Marks will depend on the quality of comment on sentence structure.

2 marks may be awarded for reference plus detailed/insightful comment; 1 mark for reference plus more basic comment; 0 marks for reference alone. Thus 4 marks could be gained as 2 + 2 or 2 + 1 + 1 or 1 + 1 + 1 + 1.

Possible answers are shown in the 'Additional guidance' column. | 4 | Possible answers include:
• list ('fan hysteria … vein for') suggests the extent of the excitement the finale generated
• 'forget trying' – direct address to the reader suggests *Breaking Bad* is so special, the writer is prepared to be daring
• dash (line 12) creates a dramatic pause before the bold claim that a TV series is on the same level as one of the most revered writers of all time
• structure of 'This is writing … the viewer' suggests a methodical, calculated approach, that the programme makers are confident, self-assured
• dash (line 16) introduces a detailed list of the calculated, successful Dickensian method with which *Breaking Bad* is being compared
• 'And, of course …' creates a rather colloquial tone with which to introduce the entrepreneurial skills of both Dickens and *Breaking Bad*
• dash (line 20) creates pause before the pointed afterthought that Dickens had an eye on the commercial potential of Christmas
• the parenthetical reference to the *Breaking Bad* box set is a light-hearted conclusion showing just how much the two have in common

or any other acceptable answer. |
| 3. | a) | **Re-read lines 22–34. Explain in your own words the reasons the writer gives for considering *Breaking Bad* to be 'art'.**

Candidates should explain the reasons the writer gives for considering *Breaking Bad* to be 'art'.

Candidates must use their own words. No marks are awarded for verbatim quotations from the passage.

1 mark for each point from the 'Additional guidance' column. | 3 | Possible answers include:
• it has taken on a depth and quality comparable to the world's greatest dramatist (explanation of 'deepened into a drama commonly referred to as Shakespearean')
• it is (with other quality TV shows) beginning to compete with the novel as the pre-eminent form of story-telling (explanation of 'close to challenging its supremacy')
• it fulfils a key requirement of art to explore the times we live in (explanation of 'express and analyse the spirit of the age')
• it is able to open up, dig deep into, rip apart and make people uneasy about the culture in which they live (explanation of 'eviscerate the society from which it emanated')

or any other acceptable answer. |

Marking guidelines for Part Four

3.	b)	Re-read lines 22–34. Analyse how the writer's imagery in lines 30–34 conveys the power of recent US TV dramas. Candidates should analyse how the writer's imagery conveys the power of recent US TV dramas. Marks will depend on the quality of comment on imagery. 2 marks may be awarded for reference plus detailed/insightful comment; 1 mark for reference plus more basic comment; 0 marks for reference alone. Thus 4 marks could be gained as 2 + 2 or 2 + 1 + 1 or 1 + 1 + 1 + 1. *Possible answers are shown in the 'Additional guidance' column.*	4	Possible answers include: • 'pinnacle' – just as the pinnacle is the highest point of a roof or tower, so *Breaking Bad* is the leader among a range of high-quality US TV drama • 'march' – just as a march is the purposeful advance of soldiers, so US TV in the last 10 years has moved forward with great strength and purpose • 'elevate' – just as to elevate is to raise up to a higher level, so TV is about to rise to the highest level: art • 'eviscerate' – just as to eviscerate is to disembowel an animal, so art (in the form of *Breaking Bad* and other TV dramas) ruthlessly opens up society or any other acceptable answer.
4.		'people interpret it in many different ways as they start to co-opt it to fit their own worldview' (lines 37–38). Explain in your own words the evidence provided for this statement in lines 35–46. Candidates should explain in their own words the evidence the writer provides for the statement that 'People interpret it in many different ways as they start to co-opt it to fit their own worldview.' Candidates must use their own words. No marks are awarded for verbatim quotations from the passage. *1 mark for each point from the 'Additional guidance' column.*	2	Possible answers include: • people in communist China see it as proof that capitalist America is corrupt, immoral (explanation of 'proves the degeneracy of America') • some Christians in the USA see the conclusion as support for their strict ethical stance on good and evil (explanation of 'a rather black-and-white morality') or any other acceptable answer.
5.	a)	Re-read lines 47–57. Explain why the writer thinks *Breaking Bad* is 'subversive' (line 47). Candidates should explain in their own words why the writer thinks *Breaking Bad* is 'subversive'. Candidates must use their own words. No marks are awarded for verbatim quotations from the passage. *1 mark for each point from the 'Additional guidance' column.*	2	Possible answers include: • it challenges, criticises the dominant political philosophy in America (explanation of 'capitalism … it will eat you up and spit you out; it will destroy you') • it challenges views of the male in society as confident/successful, presenting him instead as susceptible to violent reactions in the face of weakness (explanation of 'the state of modern masculinity … do anything to even the score') or any other acceptable answer.

Marking guidelines for Part Four

5.	b)	Re-read lines 47–57. Explain in your own words why the writer thinks Walter White is a 'tragic character' (line 55). Candidates should explain in their own words why the writer thinks Walter White is a 'tragic character'. Candidates must use their own words. No marks are awarded for verbatim quotations from the passage. *1 mark for each point from the 'Additional guidance' column.*	2	Possible answers include: • he is the cause of his own downfall (explanation of 'his own nemesis'; 'the agent of his own ruin') • despite his apparent intelligence he is unaware of himself (explanation of 'smart, but he doesn't see the truth about himself') • he only reaches self-awareness when he can do nothing to save himself (explanation of 'until it is too late') or any other acceptable answer.
6.		**Both writers express their views about *Breaking Bad*. Identify key areas on which they agree.** Candidates should identify key areas of agreement in the two passages. There may be some overlap among the areas of agreement. Markers will have to judge the extent to which a candidate has covered two points or one. Candidates can use bullet points in this final question, or write a number of linked statements. Evidence from the passage may include quotations, but these should be supported by explanations. *Approach to marking is shown in the 'Additional guidance' column.* *Key areas of agreement are shown in the grid below. Other answers are possible.*	5	The mark for this question should reflect the quality of response in two areas: • identification of the key areas of agreement in attitude/ideas • level of detail given in support The following guidelines should be used: • **5 marks** – identification of three key areas of agreement with insightful use of supporting evidence • **4 marks** – identification of three key areas of agreement with appropriate use of supporting evidence • **3 marks** – identification of three key areas of agreement • **2 marks** – identification of two key areas of agreement • **1 mark** – identification of one key area of agreement • **0 marks** – failure to identify one key area of agreement and/or misunderstanding of task

	Area of agreement	Neil Mackay	Jenny McCartney
1.	Highly praised, successful	• acclaim from fans, critics; envied by other producers ('crescendo of fan hysteria, media hype, five-star critical adoration, and ratings studio chiefs would open a vein for')	• several references, e.g. 'enormously successful series in America', 'burning question … tormenting aficionados', 'critical acclaim for *Breaking Bad*'
2.	Its addictive power	• comparison with Dickens, who 'hooked his public … punters hanging on his every word'	• some fans 'become obsessed' • writer was 'hooked too' • before finale fans were 'suspended in a state of high anticipation'
3.	Quality of drama	• many references, e.g. 'powerful, believable characters', 'places them in a contemporary, realistic setting'	• the narrative has the power to 'nail viewers to seats, while making us care about characters we might once only have despised'

4.	Status as art	• it is challenging the novel • it does what all good art does: digs deeply into society and exposes its flaws ('eviscerate the society from which it emanated') • it can be interpreted in different ways by different people • it is 'subversive and dangerous'	• it is challenging cinema as an art form • no longer thought inferior to cinema
5.	Main character's development	• his descent from ordinary family man to the 'sulphurous depths of evil' • comparison with Macbeth	• many references, e.g. 'abandons the light for the darkness', 'how badness can creep into a man's character … until it has slowly consumed him from the inside, leaving only a hollow where the soul should be', 'the inexorable direction is towards the heart of darkness', 'Walter White's dramatic trajectory'
6.	Main character as tragic hero	• brings about his own end; despite intelligence, unable to see his fate until it is too late; 'his own nemesis …'	• can't see what is happening to him, but audience can ('Walter seems oblivious to the takeover – but we can see it')
7.	Commenting on society	• various references, e.g. 'deconstruct our society', 'express and analyse the spirit of the age', 'says something very dark about American capitalism'	• the story is a caricature/parable of a key aspect of US society, about the virtues of hard work and making money ('dark parody of the American dream of enterprise and reward')
8.	Moral values ultimately upheld	• mentions, although doesn't explicitly endorse, an underlying moral code: 'what some critics saw as a rather black-and-white morality, with evil punished, good rewarded and those in need of redemption redeemed'	• asserts that moral values underpin the series ('It is also a highly moral one', 'eschews didacticism but remembers that moral arguments are the most exciting ones audiences can have')

PAPER 3 – CONSERVATION

MARKING INSTRUCTIONS FOR EACH QUESTION

Question		Expected response	Max mark	Additional guidance
1.		**Analyse how the writer's use of language in lines 1–3 creates a negative impression of 'the world of nature conservation'.** Candidates should analyse how the writer's use of language creates a negative impression of 'the world of nature conservation'. Marks will depend on the quality of comment on appropriate language feature(s). 2 marks may be awarded for reference plus detailed/insightful comment; 1 mark for reference plus more basic comment; 0 marks for reference alone. *Possible answers are shown in the 'Additional guidance' column.*	3	Possible answers include: • 'lurches' suggests movement that is uncontrolled, unplanned • 'dangerously' suggests hazardous, risky • 'lunacy' suggests extreme stupidity • contrast between '(should be to) conserve' and '(All too often …) inventing' reveals deviation from correct purpose • 'inventing' suggests creating something false, misleading • repetition of 'heritage' (balance between 'our natural heritage' and 'heritage all of its own') emphasises how wrong their approach is • 'it finds itself' suggests it happens almost randomly, without planning • 'all of its own' suggests they think/live apart from the real world or any other acceptable answer.
2.	a)	**Re-read lines 4–25. In your own words, identify two reasons given by SNH for the reintroduction of the beavers.** Candidates should identify the reasons given by SNH for the reintroduction of the beavers. Candidates must use their own words. No marks are awarded for verbatim quotations from the passage. *1 mark for each point from the 'Additional guidance' column.*	2	Possible answers include: • because it wants to establish whether or not it is a viable idea that could be extended (explanation of 'pilot project to see whether they can be introduced more widely') • because they used to be native to Britain and should be restored (explanation of 'once common in Britain, and that it would be nice to have them back') • because it is following an EU rule about reintroducing animals that have died out (explanation of 'requires member states to reintroduce extinct species.') • because it wants to promote the idea of increasing the range of wildlife in an area (explanation of 'serve to raise wider biodiversity issues') or any other acceptable answer.

Marking guidelines for Part Four

2.	b)	**Re-read lines 4–25. Explain in your own words why the writer does not approve of the project.** Candidates should explain in their own words why the writer does not approve of the project. Candidates must use their own words. No marks are awarded for verbatim quotations from the passage. *1 mark for each point from the 'Additional guidance' column.*	4	Possible answers include: • he finds the EU rule unconvincing and hard to follow (explanation of 'language seems obscure, let alone the intent behind it') • there may be some sense in restoring animals that disappeared in recent times (explanation of 'I can understand the arguments … extinct') … • … but it is a long time since there have been beavers in Britain (explanation of 'date back to the 16th century') • its demise was for understandable, practical reasons (explanation of 'a threat to local economies') • since beavers were last common, the ecology of Britain has changed beyond recognition (explanation of 'clothed in forests, with wolves, bears and other wild animals roaming the land') • bringing them back now would be too extreme a step (explanation of 'huge ecological leap back') or any other acceptable answer.
2.	c)	**Re-read lines 4–25. Analyse how the writer's use of language in lines 21–25 emphasises his disagreement.** Candidates should analyse how the writer's use of language emphasises his disagreement. Marks will depend on the quality of comment on appropriate language feature(s). 2 marks may be awarded for reference plus detailed/insightful comment; 1 mark for reference plus more basic comment; 0 marks for reference alone. Thus 4 marks could be gained as 2 + 2 or 2 + 1 + 1 or 1 + 1 + 1 + 1. *Possible answers are shown in the 'Additional guidance' column.*	4	Possible answers include: • dash introduces a specific example of the kind of reintroduction he thinks is acceptable • 'But' at the start of the sentence flags up opposing argument about the unacceptability of the beavers scheme • 'huge' suggests he thinks it is massive, unacceptably big • 'leap' suggests a movement that is unnecessarily extreme, possibly dangerous (hint of 'leap in the dark') • 'perverse' suggests it is unreasonable, wilful, abnormal • structure of 'seems … if not …' shows he thinks it is even worse than the first description • 'insane' suggests utterly senseless, deranged • contrast/balance of 'Then … Today' highlights the changes in landscape/wildlife that make this scheme so unsuitable or any other acceptable answer.
3.		**Identify in your own words the key differences in point of view between SNH and local people given in lines 26–37.** Candidates should identify in their own words the key differences in point of view between SNH and local people. Candidates must use their own words. No marks are awarded for verbatim quotations from the passage. *1 mark for each point from the 'Additional guidance' column.*	4	Possible answers include: **SNH:** • it will be good for the animals and birds of the area (explanation of 'positive impact upon local wildlife') • it will generate visitors and bring income to the area (explanation of 'tourism attractions for local economies') • it is supported by the local community (explanation of '73 per cent of the people of mid-Argyll support the idea')

Marking guidelines for Part Four

				Locals: • no evidence of support, widespread objections (explanation of 'Quite who constitutes … is unclear' or 'No local … has ever supported the project') • dismayed, shocked at the prospect of it (explanation of 'views the imminent arrival of the beavers with horror') • can't understand SNH's thinking (explanation of 'baffled') • convinced/can prove that it will be detrimental to the environment (explanation of 'can only damage' or reference to extensive evidence provided) or any other acceptable answer.
4.		**Explain ways in which, according to the writer, the RSPB is behaving like 'most conservation bodies'. Use your own words in your answer.** Candidates should explain in their own words in what ways, according to the writer, the RSPB is behaving like 'most conservation bodies'. Candidates must use their own words. No marks are awarded for verbatim quotations from the passage. *1 mark for each point from the 'Additional guidance' column.*	2	Possible answers include: • they pay no attention to any opposition (explanation of 'discount objections from people who live in the countryside') • even the protests of people directly involved are ignored (explanation of 'despite the objections of farmers … lambs') • they are unconcerned that the countryside is facing financial problems (explanation of 'when rural economies are under such pressure') • they go ahead with schemes that are or appear trivial (explanation of 'conservation projects, whose objectives seem frivolous, should be pursued') • their defence of their projects can be irrational, hard to follow (reference to 'febrile logic') … • … such that what they say can appear not just silly but reckless (explanation of 'frivolous, but irresponsible as well') or any other acceptable answer.
5	a)	**Explain how the example of the RSPB man's 'fulmars' speech is used to develop the writer's argument.** Candidates should explain how the example of the RSPB man's 'fulmar' speech is used to develop the writer's argument. Candidates must use their own words. No marks are awarded for verbatim quotations from the passage. *2 marks may be awarded for detailed/insightful comment; 1 mark for more basic comment; 0 marks for reference alone.* *Possible answers are shown in the 'Additional Guidance' column.*	2	Possible answers include: • the writer's argument that the conservationists are illogical/misguided is illustrated by the 'fulmar' example: irony that the RSPB man seems to be suggesting that the death of fulmars is acceptable (when they need/deserve to be protected) in his eagerness to defend the sea eagles against farmers' accusations about lambs • the writer's argument that conservationists' aims make no sense: fulmars, beautiful native birds, are expendable in order to provide food for incomer predators or any other acceptable answer.

Marking guidelines for Part Four

| 5. | b) | **Re-read lines 38–50. Analyse how the writer's use of language in lines 42–50 makes clear his contempt for conservation projects and the people behind them.**

Candidates should analyse how the writer's use of language makes clear his contempt for conservation projects and the people behind them.

Marks will depend on the quality of comment on appropriate language feature(s).

2 marks may be awarded for reference plus detailed/insightful comment; 1 mark for reference plus more basic comment; 0 marks for reference alone. Thus 4 marks could be gained as 2 + 2 or 2 + 1 + 1 or 1 + 1 + 1 + 1.

Possible answers are shown in the 'Additional guidance' column. | 4 | Possible answers include:
• 'perverse' suggests unreasonable, wilful, abnormal
• 'frivolous' suggests trivial, lacking substance
• 'pursued' (though it can be used in a neutral way) suggests a determination to press ahead regardless
• dash creates dramatic pause before additional condemnation, this time of the weak thinking behind the idea
• 'febrile' suggests crazed, twisted
• 'came out with' suggests a clever trick, introducing unexpected arguments
• 'startling' suggests the argument was bizarre, almost incredible
• colon introduces detailed explanation of what made the argument 'startling' – the way it dismissed claims that one species was at risk while admitting another one was being attacked
• incredulous tone in 'Yet here was …', as if to say 'Believe it or not …'
• contemptuous tone in 'little more than a larder', as if the RSPB had no concern for fulmars
• structure 'not just … but … as well' suggests they are doubly wrong
• 'irresponsible' suggests thoughtless, reckless, foolish

or any other acceptable answer. |
| 6. | | **Both writers express their views about the behaviour of nature conservation organisations. Identify key areas on which they agree. In your answer, you should refer in detail to both passages. You may answer this question in continuous prose or in a series of developed bullet points.**

Candidates should identify key areas of agreement in the two passages.

There may be some overlap among the areas of agreement. Markers will have to judge the extent to which a candidate has covered two points or one.

Candidates can use bullet points in this final question, or write a number of linked statements.

Evidence from the passage may include quotations, but these should be supported by explanations.

Approach to marking is shown in the 'Additional guidance' column.

Key areas of agreement are shown in the grid below. Other answers are possible. | 5 | The mark for this question should reflect the quality of response in two areas:
• identification of the key areas of agreement in attitude/ideas
• level of detail given in support

The following guidelines should be used:
• **5 marks** – identification of three key areas of agreement with insightful use of supporting evidence
• **4 marks** – identification of three key areas of agreement with appropriate use of supporting evidence
• **3 marks** – identification of three key areas of agreement
• **2 marks** – identification of two key areas of agreement
• **1 mark** – identification of one key area of agreement
• **0 marks** – failure to identify one key area of agreement and/or misunderstanding of task |

Marking guidelines for Part Four

	Area of agreement	Magnus Linklater	Libby Purves
1.	Not genuinely pursuing conservation	• they are ignoring their proper purpose, imposing their version of heritage ('inventing a heritage all of its own')	• they are not conserving, they are directing things, setting their own agenda, getting in the way ('fiddling, initiating, interfering')
2.	Their projects are based on a false premise	• beavers long extinct in Scotland – last recorded here 500 years ago	• sea eagles long extinct in Britain – maybe since 18th century, maybe since Roman times
3.	Disregard of environmental changes since extinction	• at the time beavers last lived here there was extensive forestation, wild animals; now cleared for farming	• at the time of extinction Britain 'was a wild, boggy, scantily occupied place'; now much more populated
4.	Original extinction came about for logical reasons applicable at the time	• beavers' destruction of trees and river banks threatened local economy, so they were killed off, driven out as farming land extended and trees cleared	• sea eagles posed a threat to farmers' livelihoods so were killed or driven to unpopulated areas
5.	Dismissal of local objections	• those with close connections to the land are far from enthusiastic about the scheme, yet SNC is deaf to objections	• strong local objections to the plan; fears for livestock, etc., yet Natural England seems determined to counter any objections
6.	Self-serving use of statistics	• figure of '73 per cent' seems not to have any basis in fact	• the claim of 'vast' popular support has little validity without knowing what question was asked
7.	Suspicion that motives are to promote the organisation to the public	• the references to 'nose-twitching, undoubtedly endearing creatures' and 'it would be nice to have them back'	• contents of the email show it is about PR for Natural England: 'flagship species', 'highlight the organisation'

PAPER 4 – SOCIAL NETWORKING

MARKING INSTRUCTIONS FOR EACH QUESTION

Question	Expected response	Max mark	Additional guidance
1.	**Identify in your own words three reasons the writer gives in lines 1–11 for the attraction of social networking.** Candidates should identify in their own words three reasons the writer gives for the attraction of social networking. Candidates must use their own words. No marks are awarded for verbatim quotations from the passage. *1 mark for each point from the 'Additional guidance' column.*	3	Possible answers include: • it eliminates the (alleged) dangers of the outside world (explanation of 'constraints of modern life … is now perceived as too dangerous') • it allows easy exchange of views/ideas among 'friends' (explanation of 'freedom of interaction and communication') • it allows a sense of belonging to a band of friends (explanation of 'basic human need to belong') • it gives a means of recognition of 'self' (explanation of 'individuals can identify themselves, making them feel important and accepted') • it is available quickly/whenever you want it (explanation of 'instant feedback and recognition … 24 hours a day.') or any other acceptable answer.
2.	**Analyse how the writer's word choice in lines 12–18 makes clear the difference between 'face-to-face' conversations and 'those in the cyber world'.** Candidates should analyse how the writer's word choice makes clear the difference between 'face-to-face' conversations and 'those in the cyber world'. Marks will depend on the quality of comment on word choice. For full marks there must be comment on both aspects. 2 marks may be awarded for reference plus detailed/insightful comment; 1 mark for reference plus more basic comment; 0 marks for reference alone. Thus 4 marks could be gained as 2 + 2 or 2 + 1 + 1 or 1 + 1 + 1 + 1. *Possible answers are shown in the 'Additional guidance' column.*	4	Possible answers include: **Real life:** • 'stress' suggests pressure, strain, anxiety • 'perilous' suggests extreme danger • 'sensitivity' suggests possibility of upset • 'adapt' suggests requirement to judge the suitable approach **Cyber world:** • 'constant' suggests something that can be relied on • 'reassurance' suggests calming, comforting, encouraging • 'distancing from' suggests protection, keeping at arm's length • 'chatting' suggests warm, friendly, easy-going or any other acceptable answer.

Marking guidelines for Part Four

3.		**Evaluate how effective you find the analogy in lines 19–24 in developing the writer's ideas. Refer in your answer to the ideas contained in the analogy and to the language used by the writer to express it.** Candidates should evaluate how effective they find the analogy in developing the writer's ideas, referring to the ideas contained in the analogy and to the language used by the writer to express it. Marks will depend on the quality of discussion of the ideas and of appropriate language feature(s). For full marks there must be comment on both ideas and language. 2 marks may be awarded for detailed/insightful comment; 1 mark for more basic comment; 0 marks for reference alone. Thus 4 marks could be gained as 2 + 2 or 2 + 1 + 1 or 1 + 1 + 1 + 1. *Possible answers are shown in the 'Additional guidance' column.*	4	Possible answers include: **Ideas:** • the analogy compares the difference between 'real' and 'cyber' conversation to the difference between the harsh reality of slaughtering animals and the neatly packaged meat sold in shops • it suggests that people feel more comfortable when they are protected from what is 'real' • it suggests people may even forget/not realise what is 'real' **Language:** • 'sanitised' suggests something unnaturally clean, something with any possible offence or upset removed • '(killing, skinning and) butchering' suggests a harsh, uncompromising process, a sense of cruelty, brutality • 'convenience' suggests something easy, safe, all the unpleasant aspects removed • 'recoil' suggests revulsion, shock when people realise what is actually involved • 'messiness, unpredictability' suggests the chaotic, uncontrolled nature of what is 'real' or any other acceptable answer.
4.	a)	**Re-read lines 25–39. Explain in your own words in what ways the writer believes social networking is 'a threat to young minds'.** Candidates should explain in their own words in what ways the writer believes social networking is 'a threat to young minds'. Candidates must use their own words. No marks are awarded for verbatim quotations from the passage. *1 mark for each point from the 'Additional guidance' column, but for full marks there should be attention to both key points.*	4	Possible answers include: **Key point:** It diminishes the ability to concentrate (explanation of 'attention span is at risk'). • because of the frenetic speed of on-screen exchanges (explanation of 'instant new screen images flashing up') • the brain might get used to responding without enough time to process properly (explanation of 'might accustom the brain to operate over such timescales') • it could be the cause of/connected with ADHD (reference to 'might be in some way linked …') **Key point:** It encourages concentration on the moment (explanation of 'preference for the here-and-now'). • no consideration of knock-on effects (explanation of 'the immediacy of an experience trumps any regard for the consequences') • everything is about excitement (explanation of 'the thrill of the moment, the buzz of …') • makes people more impetuous (explanation of 'impulsive') • no awareness of/consideration for others (explanation of 'solipsistic') or any other acceptable answer.

Marking guidelines for Part Four

4.	b)	**Re-read lines 25–39. Analyse how the writer's use of language in lines 33–39 conveys her disapproval of video games. You should refer in your answer to such features as word choice, tone, sentence structure …** Candidates should analyse how the writer's use of language conveys her disapproval of video games. Marks will depend on the quality of comment on appropriate language feature(s). For full marks there must be comment on at least two features. 2 marks may be awarded for reference plus detailed/insightful comment; 1 mark for reference plus more basic comment; 0 marks for reference alone. Thus 4 marks could be gained as 2 + 2 or 2 + 1 + 1 or 1 + 1 + 1 + 1. *Possible answers are shown in the 'Additional guidance' column.*	4	Possible answers include: **Word choice:** • 'here-and-now' suggests games encourage focus on the moment, without consideration of past or future • 'trumps' suggests that one thing (the present) always wins over another (the future effects) • 'thrill of the moment' suggests short-lived pleasure for its own sake • 'buzz' suggests self-indulgent, thrill-seeking • 'impulsive' suggests reckless, rash, rather selfish • 'solipsistic' suggests entirely self-centred, total lack of concern for others **Tone:** • very colloquial, dismissive; 'After all … you can always just' suggests the sloppy thinking, irresponsible attitude she thinks games produce **Sentence structure:** • dash after 'princess' introduces stark explanation focusing on the callousness induced by the games • 'No … none' – use of negatives at start and finish of sentence suggests they are empty activities, emphasises how critical she is or any other acceptable answer.
5.		**Explain in your own words why the writer makes references to a 'princess' in lines 40–45.** Candidates should explain in their own words why the writer makes references to a 'princess'. Candidates must use their own words. No marks are awarded for verbatim quotations from the passage. *1 mark for each point from the 'Additional guidance' column.*	3	Possible answers include: • to exemplify the (alleged) change in young people's ability to understand others' feelings (explanation of 'empathy' or 'how others feel and think, as distinct from oneself') • reading a novel about a princess engages the reader with the character/personality of the princess (explanation of 'the aim of … [is] to find out more about the princess herself') … • … whereas games about rescuing a princess are played in order to make the player feel good (explanation of 'the goal is to feel rewarded') or any other acceptable answer.
6.		**Analyse how the writer's use of language in lines 46–54 conveys her disapproval of social networking. In your answer you should refer to such features as tone, sentence structure, word choice …**	3	Possible answers include: **Tone:** • dry, ironic in 'it seems strange that … so concerned … are at the same time enthusiastically embracing …', as if rather politely pointing out the stupidity

Marking guidelines for Part Four

| | | Candidates should analyse how the writer's use of language conveys her disapproval of social networking.

Marks will depend on the quality of comment on appropriate language feature(s). For full marks there must be comment on at least two features.

2 marks may be awarded for reference plus detailed/insightful comment; 1 mark for reference plus more basic comment; 0 marks for reference alone.

Possible answers are shown in the 'Additional guidance' column. | | • restraint, mock-modesty in 'Are we perhaps …', when it's clear she is sure this is the case
• contemptuous, dismissive in '… however banal', describing thoughts and activities as dull, trite
• feigned ignorance/incomprehension in 'I believe it is called Twitter' creates a sense of a person from a distant generation guardedly referring to some strange modern phenomenon; tone of almost self-conscious superiority

Sentence structure:
• 'moment-by-moment, flood-of-consciousness' – list-like and exaggerated by hyphenated forms to create sense of breakneck speed, unnecessary compression
• final sentence is very flat, lifeless in contrast to previous, which is longer and more involved – creates some sense of distaste/mockery (almost self-mockery)

Word choice:
• 'fast-paced', 'instant' suggest too rapid, threatening, ultra-modern
• 'baffling' suggests bemusing, bewildering, as if designed to confuse
• 'preoccupation' suggests unhealthy excess of attention

or any other acceptable answer. |
| 7. | | **Both writers express their views about social networking. Identify key areas on which they agree.**

Candidates should identify key areas of agreement in the two passages.

There may be some overlap among the areas of agreement. Markers will have to judge the extent to which a candidate has covered two points or one.

Candidates can use bullet points in this final question, or write a number of linked statements.

Evidence from the passage may include quotations, but these should be supported by explanations.

Approach to marking is shown in the 'Additional guidance' column.

Key areas of agreement are shown in the grid below. Other answers are possible. | 5 | The mark for this question should reflect the quality of response in two areas:
• identification of the key areas of agreement in attitude/ideas
• level of detail given in support

The following guidelines should be used:
• **5 marks** – identification of three key areas of agreement with insightful use of supporting evidence
• **4 marks** – identification of three key areas of agreement with appropriate use of supporting evidence
• **3 marks** – identification of three key areas of agreement
• **2 marks** – identification of two key areas of agreement
• **1 mark** – identification of one key area of agreement
• **0 marks** – failure to identify one key area of agreement and/or misunderstanding of task |

Marking guidelines for Part Four

	Area of agreement	Baroness Greenfield	Moses Ma
1.	It fulfils an important social need	• allows easy contact regardless of space or time ('freedom of interaction and communication', 'instant feedback … from someone, somewhere – 24 hours a day.')	• provides ability to be part of a group ('feelings of community generated by your workplace, your church, your sports team', 'social needs, like those for belonging, love and affection')
2.	It fulfils an important psychological need	• allows people to express personality and be recognised by others ('identify themselves, making them feel important and accepted') • 'reassurance – that you are listened to, recognised'	• the feeling of community is a deep emotional need, especially in today's less tribal world ('a culture starved for real community', 'Our brains are wired to operate within the social context of community')
3.	It can encourage self-centredness	• loss of empathy; the princess analogies; 'such activities may result in a more impulsive and solipsistic attitude'	• it makes people believe they are centre of the universe ('unconditional narcissism', '*I tweet, therefore I am … goddammit, people like me!*')
4.	It can create a distorted view of the world	• makes traditional conversation seem difficult; the slaughterhouse analogy	• generates a belief that someone is actually interested in another's trivia ('others might actually care about the minutiae of our daily lives')
5.	It creates a distorted view of self	• the child who believed she had 900 friends; the suggestion that you might 'think about yourself differently'	• people start to feel an importance they don't really have ('to feel like celebrities')
6.	Much of what is written is trivial	• all done at speed, with no thought to its significance ('an almost moment-by-moment, flood-of-consciousness account of your thoughts and activities, however banal')	• the examples given in the third paragraph ('useless drivel')

PAPER 5 – CHRISTMAS

MARKING INSTRUCTIONS FOR EACH QUESTION

Question		Expected response	Max mark	Additional guidance
1.	a)	**Re-read lines 1–10. Explain why, according to the writer, Christmas is particularly hard for women.** Candidates should explain why, according to the writer, Christmas is particularly hard for women. Candidates must use their own words. No marks are awarded for verbatim quotations from the passage. *1 mark for each point from the 'Additional guidance' column.*	2	Possible answers include: • because the task of deciding on presents falls to them (explanation of '[choosing presents] is the almost exclusive preserve of women') • because the task of acquiring the presents falls to them (explanation of 'and actually finding it') • because they are put under great stress/have to work very hard (explanation of 'have a manic look in their eyes', 'synapses working overtime', 'hard emotional labour') • because they have to live up to a stereotype (explanation of 'expected to demonstrate those feminine skills of empathy and thoughtfulness') • because they don't get sufficient recognition for their efforts (explanation of 'with much of the credit going to a mysterious, elusive man') or any other acceptable answer.
1.	b)	**Re-read lines 1–10. By referring to more than one example, analyse how the writer creates a light-hearted tone in these lines.** Candidates should analyse how the writer creates a light-hearted tone. Marks will depend on the quality of comment on tone. For full marks there must be comment on more than one example. 2 marks may be awarded for reference plus detailed/insightful comment; 1 mark for reference plus more basic comment; 0 marks for reference alone. *Possible answers are shown in the 'Additional guidance' column.*	2	Possible answers include: • 'We're hardly capable …' – ironic, self-mocking use of first person plural, grouping all women together as incompetent • 'mulled wine and mince pies' – gentle, homely, traditional, but trivial details to contrast with (allegedly) deranged actions • 'peer into our brains' creates a comic, cartoon-like picture • '– and actually finding it' – added point after pause to emphasise humorously that it's even worse than it seems • 'burning up a power station's worth of mental energy' – hyperbolic comparison of brains to a power station running at full power • 'a mysterious, elusive man' – wry reference to Santa Claus as the male who (unfairly) gets all the thanks or any other acceptable answer.

Marking guidelines for Part Four

| 2. | a) | **Re-read lines 11–23. Identify in your own words the features of modern life that make it hard to replicate a Victorian Christmas today.**

Candidates should identify in their own words the features of modern life that make it hard to replicate a Victorian Christmas today.

Candidates must use their own words. No marks are awarded for verbatim quotations from the passage.

1 mark for each point from the 'Additional guidance' column. | 3 | Possible answers include:
• today most women work/don't stay at home, unlike women in Victorian times who had the time needed to organise the lavish Christmas celebrations (explanation of 'requiring months of preparation', 'If women were to be kept at home …')
• today everyone is expected to do it, unlike in Victorian times when it was only the better off who held lavish Christmas celebrations (explanation of 'it was only the middle classes')
• today hardly anyone has domestic servants, unlike middle-class women in Victorian times who had many (explanation of 'large amount of servant labour … the near-impossible task of putting on the show single-handed')
• today we are subject to a level of commercial pressure and increase in expectations that did not exist in Victorian times (explanation of 'consumer culture and its massive inflation of present expectations')

or any other acceptable answer. |
| 2. | b) | **Re-read lines 11–23. Analyse how the writer's word choice and sentence structure make clear her view of the Victorians and the Christmas celebrations they created.**

Candidates should analyse how the writer's word choice and sentence structure make clear her view of the Victorians and the Christmas celebrations they created.

Marks will depend on the quality of comment on appropriate language feature(s). For full marks there must be comment on both features.

2 marks may be awarded for reference plus detailed/insightful comment; 1 mark for reference plus more basic comment; 0 marks for reference alone. Thus 4 marks could be gained as 2 + 2 or 2 + 1 + 1 or 1 + 1 + 1 + 1.

Possible answers are shown in the 'Additional guidance' column. | 4 | Possible answers include:
Word choice:
• 'blame' suggests they did something wrong, have something to answer for
• 'invented' suggests made up, hint of falseness, deception
• 'ingeniously' suggests an element of craftiness, deceit
• 'turning' suggests twisting, distorting the true nature
• 'sober religious' suggests that what they replaced was noble, serious, restrained, respectful
• 'great festival' suggests something overblown, excessive
• 'fiddling' suggests petty task, purposeless action required to live up to the ideal
• 'putting on the show' suggests that attempting to live up to the Victorian model is as elaborate as mounting a theatrical production; 'show' itself suggests something artificial, put on to impress
• 'epidemic (of seasonal migraines and divorces)' suggests the pressures of trying to put on a Victorian Christmas can result in widespread suffering |

45

Marking guidelines for Part Four

				Sentence structure: • parenthesis is used to introduce a detailed description of the features of the Victorian Christmas • list ('trees …') suggests the sheer extent of the Christmas features the Victorians invented • colon introduces expansion of the claim that it 'had got worse', i.e. that the women had more demands put on their time (making trivial ornamentation) • 'But …' at the start of the paragraph forcefully signals that a significant reversal of the images in the previous paragraph is about to come or any other acceptable answer.
3.	a)	**Re-read lines 24–46. Identify in your own words the key points of the writer's argument in lines 24–37 that the 'rituals the Victorians developed for Christmas' were 'a response to industrialisation'.** Candidates should identify in their own words the key points of the writer's argument that the 'rituals the Victorians developed for Christmas' were 'a response to industrialisation'. Candidates must use their own words. No marks are awarded for verbatim quotations from the passage. *1 mark for each point from the 'Additional guidance' column.*	4	Possible answers include: • the family was no longer the core around which money was earned/produced (explanation of 'the family was no longer the wealth-producing unit') • people became part of large workforces away from the home (explanation of 'swapping work at home for factories and offices') • the expansion of cities/towns broke up existing family/community lifestyles (explanation of 'urbanisation was disrupting the old domestic structures') • as a result of all the above, something was needed to reinforce family/community ties (explanation of 'Social relations needed strengthening') • the home became romanticised as a refuge from/antidote to the forces of capitalism/industrialisation (explanation of 'Home was idealised as a sanctuary from competitive market capitalism') • there was a big focus on children living innocently, free from the pressures generated by capitalism/industrialisation (explanation of 'childhood was idealised as a life stage free of responsibility, a time of imagination, magic and enchantment') or any other acceptable answer.
3.	b)	**Re-read lines 24–46. Explain in your own words the reasons the writer gives in lines 38–46 for making a 'fuss' of Christmas.** Candidates should explain in their own words the reasons the writer gives for making a 'fuss' of Christmas. Candidates must use their own words. No marks are awarded for verbatim quotations from the passage. *1 mark for each point from the 'Additional guidance' column.*	4	Possible answers include: • to relieve/escape the pressures associated with a money-dominated world (explanation of 'the rigours of market capitalism') • to compensate for the fact that families are less likely to be together at other times (explanation of 'fragmented and dispersed families') • to be especially kind/loving to the children we see little of because we work such long hours (explanation of 'harder we work … create the perfect children's Christmas')

				• to relieve/mitigate the pressures placed on our children by the education system (explanation of 'institutionalised and regimented') • to reinforce our sense of children's purity (explanation of 'more we worry about their safety') or any other acceptable answer.
3.	c)	**Re-read lines 24–46. Analyse how the sentence structure of lines 38–46 emphasises the point that the writer is making in the paragraph.** Candidates should analyse how the sentence structure emphasises the point that the writer is making in the paragraph. Marks will depend on the quality of comment on sentence structure. For full marks the key point must be addressed. 2 marks may be awarded for reference plus detailed/insightful comment; 1 mark for reference plus more basic comment; 0 marks for reference alone. *Possible answers are shown in the 'Additional guidance' column.*	3	Possible answers include: • **Key point:** the entire paragraph is a sequence of five sentences with identical/parallel structure: 'The' plus comparative followed by 'the more we …'; the first element is a danger or a worry in our lives and the second element is our increasing need to challenge and overcome it by celebrating Christmas on a lavish scale – this structure creates an intense pattern of all the bad things we try to erase from our minds at Christmas • the list-like structure suggests just how many worries and problems we face in modern life • the parenthetical remark ('and are bitterly disappointed …') reminds us how unlikely it is that the 'dream' will be realised • the information between the dashes expands/exemplifies the idea contained in 'institutionalised and regimented' • reaches a climax in 'after news of another sickening child-abduction, we all need Christmas', juxtaposing a parent's deepest fear with the restorative power of a traditional Christmas or any other acceptable answer.
4.		**Evaluate the effectiveness of the final paragraph (lines 47–51) as a conclusion to the passage as a whole. You should refer in your answer to ideas and to language.** Candidates should discuss the effectiveness of the final paragraph as a conclusion to the passage as a whole. Marks will depend on the quality of comment. For full marks there must be comment on both ideas and language. 2 marks may be awarded for detailed/insightful comment; 1 mark for more basic comment; 0 marks for reference alone. *Possible answers are shown in the 'Additional guidance' column.*	3	Possible answers include: • criticism of the modern Christmas is continued in the metaphor 'emotional bulimia', which suggests our Christmas celebrations amount to an excess of feelings, hopes, dreams; we try to cram too much into it, expect too much from it • there are more sensible ways of celebrating, bringing families together, i.e. having several occasions throughout the year instead of investing all our efforts into one • the point argued earlier that it is all the fault of modern economic structures and pressures is reiterated in 'Anglo-Saxon capitalism disciplined the festive impulse' • the rather cynical tone at the end ('factory routine was not disrupted year-round by drunkenness') is in keeping with her earlier view that capitalism has a stranglehold on our lives or any other acceptable answer.

Marking guidelines for Part Four

5.	**Both writers express their views about the way we celebrate Christmas. Identify key areas on which they agree.** Candidates should identify key areas of agreement in the two passages. There may be some overlap among the areas of agreement. Markers will have to judge the extent to which a candidate has covered two points or one. Candidates can use bullet points in this final question, or write a number of linked statements. Evidence from the passage may include quotations, but these should be supported by explanations. *Approach to marking is shown in the 'Additional guidance' column.* *Key areas of agreement are shown in the grid below. Other answers are possible.*	5	The mark for this question should reflect the quality of response in two areas: • identification of the key areas of agreement in attitude/ideas • level of detail given in support The following guidelines should be used: • **5 marks** – identification of three key areas of agreement with insightful use of supporting evidence • **4 marks** – identification of three key areas of agreement with appropriate use of supporting evidence • **3 marks** – identification of three key areas of agreement • **2 marks** – identification of two key areas of agreement • **1 mark** – identification of one key area of agreement • **0 marks** – failure to identify one key area of agreement and/or misunderstanding of task

	Area of agreement	**Madeleine Bunting**	**Terence Blacker**
1.	**Christmas puts a great strain on families**	• the stress is felt by women in particular • reference to 'seasonal migraines and divorces'	• reference to 'Panicky family plans', Christmas as a time 'of stress and loneliness' • refers to post-Christmas as good for the lawyers who handle divorces
2.	**We seem to feel pressured into celebrating it**	• the pressure to emulate the Victorian Christmas	• describes Christmas as something we don't really look forward to, refers to it as a 'duty'
3.	**It is dominated by the pressure to spend**	• the growth of consumerism and the power of capitalism has created a 'massive inflation of present expectations'	• the issues surrounding publishing and the way Christmas distorts the book market
4.	**We expect/hope that it will solve deeper problems in our lives**	• the desire to bring fragmented families together ('the annual dream of togetherness') • the attempt to compensate children for not being able to give them enough attention at other times ('an experience of magical enchantment')	• criticises the obsession with seeing Christmas as a cure-all ('repairing fragile relationships', 'children who have been ignored can be showered with presents')

Marking guidelines for Part Four

5.	Christmas is too concentrated on just a few days in the year	• all done in 'one brief period' (instead of spread through the year)	• 'shoe-horns the demands of extended family life into a few fraught, emotional, very expensive days' • 'try to spread the giving, the time spent with family, the parties, the general bonding of relationships throughout the rest of the year'

PAPER 6 – SHOPPING

MARKING INSTRUCTIONS FOR EACH QUESTION

Question		Expected response	Max mark	Additional guidance
1.	a)	**Re-read lines 1–14. Identify in your own words the key criticisms the writer makes of the way we live today.** Candidates should identify in their own words the key criticisms the writer makes of the way we live today. Candidates must use their own words. No marks are awarded for verbatim quotations from the passage. *1 mark for each point from the 'Additional guidance' column.*	4	Possible answers include: • we are all involved in using/buying too many things (explanation of 'caught up on a treadmill of turbo-consumption') • we hope that this activity will bring contentment but find that the results are negative/unfulfilling (explanation of 'unfounded belief that having more will make us happy') • our lives are to an extent controlled by consumerism (explanation of 'predominant thing that you and I do') • our identity is no longer bound up in our jobs or the products we make (explanation of 'Once we were a society of producers') • we are defined by the goods we purchase (explanation of 'we understand ourselves and project the image we want') • we are forced into unnecessary choices (explanation of 'With every purchasing decision, they reject thousands of other options') or any other acceptable answer.
1.	b)	**Re-read lines 1–14. Analyse how the writer's word choice in lines 1–3 emphasises his low opinion of 'consumer society'.** Candidates should analyse how the writer's word choice emphasises his low opinion of 'consumer society'. Marks will depend on the quality of comment on word choice. 2 marks may be awarded for reference plus detailed/insightful comment; 1 mark for reference plus more basic comment; 0 marks for reference alone. *Possible answers are shown in the 'Additional guidance' column.*	2	Possible answers include: • 'caught up' suggests trapped, unable to escape • 'treadmill' suggests relentless, unable to get off • 'turbo-consumption' suggests super-charged, difficult to control, too powerful • 'powered' suggests forceful, controlling • 'unfounded' suggests illusory, misguided • 'part and parcel' suggests packaged like a business commodity • 'tarnished' suggests tainted, contaminated or any other acceptable answer.

Marking guidelines for Part Four

1.	c)	**Re-read lines 1–14. Analyse how the writer creates a critical tone in lines 9–14 about those who say they are 'above fashion'.** Candidates should analyse how the writer creates a critical tone about those who say they are 'above fashion'. Marks will depend on the quality of comment on tone. 2 marks may be awarded for reference plus detailed/insightful comment; 1 mark for reference plus more basic comment; 0 marks for reference alone. *Possible answers are shown in the 'Additional guidance' column.*	2	Possible answers include: • 'pretend' suggests they are being deceitful and/or deluding themselves • 'finely calibrated' suggests they make unnecessarily elaborate decisions • 'reject thousands' exaggerates the extent of their decision-making • 'on other … in other' suggests a sort of frantic movement around the shops • 'home in on' depicts them as single-minded, almost predatory • inverted commas around 'them' mocks the stupidity/pretentiousness of claiming affinity with an object • inverted commas around 'fashion' ridicules the fashions of the masses as compared with their own more specialist preferences • '*their* fashion' mocks their possessiveness, sense of exclusiveness • the parallel/antithetical structure of the last sentence (reversing subject and predicate) suggests how for some people 'things' have gained the upper hand or any other acceptable answer.
2.	a)	**Re-read lines 15–20. According to the writer, what two key aspects of our lives do we attempt to satisfy by 'running on the consumer treadmill'?** Candidates should say what two key aspects of our lives we attempt to satisfy by 'running on the consumer treadmill'. Candidates must use their own words. No marks are awarded for verbatim quotations from the passage. *1 mark for each point from the 'Additional guidance' column.*	2	Possible answers include: • the spiritual/emotional (explanation of 'freedom, escape, love, care, excitement and comfort') • prestige, being better than others (explanation of 'status') or any other acceptable answer.
2.	b)	**Re-read lines 15–20. Analyse how the writer's sentence structure in these lines emphasises the points he is making.** Candidates should analyse how the writer's sentence structure emphasises the points he is making. Marks will depend on the quality of comment on sentence structure. 2 marks may be awarded for reference plus detailed/insightful comment; 1 mark for reference plus more basic comment; 0 marks for reference alone. Thus 4 marks could be gained as 2 + 2 or 2 + 1 + 1 or 1 + 1 + 1 + 1. *Possible answers are shown in the 'Additional guidance' column.*	4	Possible answers include: • question emphasises desire to explain the compulsion • list ('freedom, escape …') suggests how many things we try to achieve via consumerism • repetition of 'We buy …' to suggest the continuous, never-ending process • use of 'And' at the start of a sentence (non-standard, grammatically incorrect for many) draws attention to the point, as if saying 'last but not least' • 'And, of course, we buy status.' – short, declarative, abrupt sentence focuses attention on what seems to be the most significant idea

Marking guidelines for Part Four

				• list ('to be … to covet … to wear') suggests the huge number of things we hope to achieve via consumerism • repetition/list of superlatives ('best', 'newest', 'latest') emphasises the obsession with outdoing others or any other acceptable answer.
3.		**Analyse how the writer's imagery in lines 21–25 conveys his view of how 'The whole show' is organised.** Candidates should analyse how the writer's imagery conveys his view of how 'The whole show' is organised. Marks will depend on the quality of comment on imagery. 2 marks may be awarded for reference plus detailed/insightful comment; 1 mark for reference plus more basic comment; 0 marks for reference alone. Thus 4 marks could be gained as 2 + 2 or 2 + 1 + 1 or 1 + 1 + 1 + 1. *Possible answers are shown in the 'Additional guidance' column.*	4	Possible answers include: • 'laboratory' – just as a laboratory is used by scientific experts for conducting experiments, so the retail industry is constantly exploring new ways of promoting/selling products • 'machinery' – just as machinery is used to manufacture goods, so the retail industry uses the results of their research to build an image for their products • 'factory' – just as a factory is used for the manufacture of physical goods, so the image of products and our desire for them is constructed with the same industrial focus • 'engineering' – just as engineering involves the skilful fine-tuning of objects, so the retail industry is constantly refining the way we are encouraged to be consumers or any other acceptable answer.
4.		**According to the writer in lines 37–41, what are the problems with our dependence on 'retail therapy' and what solutions does he suggest?** Candidates should give the problems with our dependence on 'retail therapy' and the solutions the writer suggests. Candidates must use their own words. No marks are awarded for verbatim quotations from the passage. *1 mark for each point from the 'Additional guidance' column.*	4	Possible answers include: **Problems:** • ultimately it disappoints, because more is never enough • the fewer mental/spiritual resources we have to fall back on, the more we need to buy things; but this doesn't really fill the gap, so we need to buy more • shopping only works well enough for us to want to buy more, which just creates a never-ending cycle of unsatisfactory buying **Solutions:** • get things in perspective (explanation of 'strike a balance') • stop letting the retail industry control us (explanation of 'regaining control over a marketing machine') • adopt a more purposeful view of what life should be about (explanation of 'a more compelling vision of what it means to be free and live a good life') • come to understand that the important things in life are not for sale (explanation of 'grasp the fact that what we really need and cherish can't be bought') or any other acceptable answer.

Marking guidelines for Part Four

5.		**By referring to lines 42–52, identify in your own words the three measures the writer suggests the Government should take to 'help us rebalance our lives'.**	3	Possible answers include:
		Candidates should identify in their own words the three measures the writer suggests the Government should take to 'help us rebalance our lives'.		<ul><li>stop advertisements aimed at children</li><li>put up taxes on expensive items that are bought for status only</li><li>measure how contented the people in the country feel, not how much money they have</li></ul>or any other acceptable answer.
		Candidates must use their own words. No marks are awarded for verbatim quotations from the passage.		
		1 mark for each point from the 'Additional guidance' column.		
6.		**Both writers express their views about consumerism. Identify key areas on which they agree and on which they disagree.**	5	The mark for this question should reflect the quality of response in two areas:<ul><li>identification of the key differences and similarities in attitude/ideas</li><li>level of detail given in support</li></ul>To score 2 or more marks, there must be at least one area of agreement and one area of disagreement. The following guidelines should be used:<ul><li>**5 marks** – identification of three key areas of agreement and disagreement with insightful use of supporting evidence</li><li>**4 marks** – identification of three key areas of agreement and disagreement with appropriate use of supporting evidence</li><li>**3 marks** – identification of three key areas of agreement and disagreement</li><li>**2 marks** – identification of two key areas of agreement and disagreement</li><li>**1 mark** – identification of one key area of agreement or disagreement</li><li>**0 marks** – failure to identify one key area of agreement and disagreement and/or misunderstanding of task</li></ul>
		Candidates should identify key areas of agreement and disagreement in the two passages.		
		There may be some overlap among the areas of agreement. Markers will have to judge the extent to which a candidate has covered two points or one.		
		Candidates can use bullet points in this final question, or write a number of linked statements.		
		Evidence from the passage may include quotations, but these should be supported by explanations.		
		Approach to marking is shown in the 'Additional guidance' column.		
		Key areas of agreement and disagreement are shown in the grids overleaf. Other answers are possible.		

Marking guidelines for Part Four

	Area of agreement	Neal Lawson	Deyan Sudjic
1.	Consumerism is a powerful force	• it dominates every aspect of our lives; we are judged by what we own/buy • has reversed the relationship between people and consumer goods ('We don't own things – they own us') • it is a relentless force ('It is the most vicious of vicious circles')	• his experience of buying a new laptop; admits it was almost beyond his control ('the laptop that eventually persuaded me that I had to have it did it all by itself') • refers elsewhere to 'an ecstatic consumerist trance'
2.	A key tactic is to create a desire for the newest model	• the 'factory' metaphor – a whole industry geared to making us believe we need things that we don't ('engineering new wants into new needs: more and more things we must have') • the whole idea is 'not to make us satisfied but dissatisfied, so that we soon go back for more'	• nothing wrong with his old laptop, but it will be dumped; when bought, it was highly desirable ('the most desirable, and most knowing piece of technology that I could ever have wanted') • description of Apple as compelling customers to buy new products ('so hungry for a new product that they will throw away the last one every two years')
3.	Purchases can be motivated by 'aspirational' feelings	• desire for status, wanting to have the best of everything • people let themselves be judged by their purchases ('who and what they are and what they want others to think of them')	• his new laptop 'looked sleek, technocratic and composed' (i.e. the way certain people might want to look to create an impression) • also: 'Black has been used over the years … to suggest seriousness', 'use design as a lure to turn its product into aspirational alternatives'

	Area of disagreement	Neal Lawson	Deyan Sudjic
4.	Influence of consumerism on society	• malignant, damaging force that makes us buy things we don't need • distorts true happiness ('unfounded belief that having more will make us happy')	• no overt criticism; admits he's being manipulated but enjoys the experience, and knows he'll come back for more
5.	Who's to blame	• everyone involved in the 'vast laboratory'	• ourselves, for being so easily seduced
6.	Need for action	• government intervention; change of whole societal outlook	• no action needed – just enjoy the beauty of the objects